Contents

G000022631

WITHDRAWN FROM STOCK

DATE .... INITIALS ....

London Institute 52; The Cookery and Food
Association 53; The Hotel & Catering Training
Company 54; The Hotel Catering & Institutional
Management Association 55; Confederation of
Tourism, Hotel and Catering Management 56;
European Catering Association (Great Britain) 57;
Institute of Home Economics 57; National
Examinations Board for Supervisory Management
57; Royal Institute of Public Health and Hygiene 58;
Royal Society of Health 58; Institute of Food Science
and Technology 59; The Wine and Spirit Education
Trust Ltd 59; The British Institute of Innkeeping 60;
Caterer & Hotelkeeper 61

Part 2

Introduction

When you order a meal in a restaurant or hotel, have you ever considered the number of people involved in preparing your food? There are the chef and his assistants who do the cooking, the waiter or waitress who serves you, the wine waiter who provides you with something to drink, and possibly the receptionist or cashier who takes your money afterwards, and may have reserved you a seat first. Even in a small restaurant or café more than one person is involved in providing a meal.

The catering industry is immense. It comprises industrial, institutional, and contract catering – some factories as well as schools and hospitals have their own catering departments, but often facilities are by contract caterer – hotels, restaurants and cafés; ships, railways and airways; the armed forces; private catering for wedding receptions or similar gatherings; small public house bars which serve sandwiches.

Caterers are also involved in the production of chilled and frozen convenience foods, now an expanding market. New university courses in Food Science and Technology, such as that at the University of Humberside, are designed to prepare students for careers in the food industry, with an emphasis on modern food processing and large-scale food manufacture.

Tourism and leisure is now one of the fastest growing areas of employment within the British economy, particularly in the licensed trade, restaurants and retail catering, together with tourism facilities. There are plenty of opportunities for a career in the industry, especially in the south-east, in both catering and hotel management.

This book attempts to describe all the different careers available. It is intended particularly for school and college leavers, who may be uncertain about how to begin a career in catering. They should be aware that they may have to work unsocial hours and in conditions that the average office worker would shun. Some kitchens, for example, do not always have outside windows and rely on extractors and artificial lighting. Sometimes pay is low and hours are long. However, the only way to find out what really is involved is to take part. Catering is something that goes on every day, not just Monday to Friday and certainly not just 9 am to 5 pm, although if you are under 16 there are restrictions on the number of hours you can work. If you are the sort of person who would be bored sitting behind a desk and do not want to work the same hours every day, then catering might be the career for you.

There is no easy way to start a catering career. Some people obtain weekend jobs or work in the school holidays, and then after leaving school continue to work at that establishment.

Part 1

Chapter 1

Hotels and Restaurants

The catering industry, including hotel management, is one of the largest in the country. There is great variety in the industry. In this chapter, under the heading of hotels and restaurants, are included:

- Hotels and restaurants
- Motels and motorway service stations
- Steak bars and cafés
- Holiday camps and leisure centres
- Public houses, clubs and inns
- Fast food shops.

Some of the units are very small – just a team of people operating under the proprietor, who may have his family working for him. New restaurants spring up sometimes where the owners have all worked together previously for someone else, but have pooled their savings and launched out on their own.

There are many job opportunities in catering, whether experienced or not, but experienced staff naturally can claim better wages and are more likely to get the best jobs. In a large hotel there are many specialist occupations, from head porter, barman and seamstress to chef rôtisseur and wine waiter.

The front-of-the-house staff, some of whom are uniformed, are the first contact with the guests and therefore give the first impression of the establishment; kitchen staff rarely see the guests. Waiters get to know their customers personally – they often recognise them after several years' absence – and the person who goes to the same hotel year after year may often be on friendly terms with the waiter.

Management and Catering Staff in a Large Hotel

Hotel Manager

Hotel management is a very demanding occupation. In Part 2 the various degree and other courses in management are listed, but not everyone enters with a relevant qualification; many people from other professions and careers have turned very successfully to hotel management. The ability to plan and control, financial skills, and a knowledge of food, drink, and accommodation services are required. Managers must be prepared to promote technological change, should be good mixers and get on well with their staff and guests. Another essential is an ability to select the right staff at all levels. They should also have stamina and be prepared to work hard and for long hours.

In a large hotel the general manager will be helped by a controller, who may also be an assistant manager; he will be in charge of the day-to-day management of the hotel finances, stock ordering, and supervising the storekeepers.

Training

School leavers start the process of training for hotel management by taking A levels and doing a BTEC/SCOTVEC or specialised degree course at one of the universities or colleges of higher education. Some hotel groups take on trainee managers (see Chapter 12), and the students study for Business and Technology Education Council (BTEC) qualifications at their local further education college. From 1993/94, BTEC qualifications will be overtaken by NVQs (see page 17).

There are three levels of BTEC qualification:

1. *BTEC First courses in Hotel and Catering Studies.* These are designed to lay the foundations for progress to national level studies. The programmes prepare students for a range of jobs in catering, hospitals, hotels, leisure centres, residential homes and restaurants and take one year part time (course fees are normally paid by the student's employer). Each course contains core subjects plus optional subjects. The core subjects are:

   Introduction to the Hotel and Catering Industry: provides a background to the industry, and awareness of aspects such as health, safety and hygiene. It helps students to develop confidence in dealing with customers and colleagues, and understand planning and controlling costs.

Introduction to Food Preparation and Service: covers buying, storing, preparing, presenting and servicing food and drink.

The Clean Environment: basic skills for a range of cleaning operations; the importance of a clean, hygienic and safe environment.

Different colleges offer different optional subjects. Those available include:

Catering in restaurants
Catering for vegetarians
Cleaning operations
Food and drink service
Food preparation
Front office work
Hotel and catering costing and control
Nutrition
Languages.

Some colleges allow specialisation in accommodation services or hotel reception. Over 180 colleges run BTEC First courses in Hotel and Catering; a list is available from careers teachers or advisory services, or from BTEC Information Services.

BTEC First Certificate courses are normally part time for one year. First Diploma courses are full time for one year, or part time for two years. BTEC certificate and diploma courses are equal in standard and status, but the diploma courses include more option subjects and can lead to a wider choice of careers.

2. *BTEC National courses in Hotel, Catering and Institutional Operations.* These are designed for young people who intend to work, or are already working, in the industry. They lead to a choice of careers in the commercial, welfare and institutional sectors, including airlines, catering companies, hospitals, hotels, leisure centres, passenger ships and restaurants. Jobs include accommodation supervisor, bar manager, catering officer, head receptionist, housekeeper, kitchen supervisor and restaurant supervisor. Core subjects are:

The Hotel and Catering Industry: the structure of organisations in the industry and how they are run in a cost-effective way; also customer care.

Hotel and Catering in Context: the relationship between the industry and tourism and leisure; includes sales and marketing skills, and legal aspects of the industry.

Hotel and Catering Administration: develops skills and knowledge needed for running an office, including keyboarding and computing skills.

People at Work: develops ability and confidence for dealing with customers and colleagues.

Applied Science: applies scientific principles to nutrition, food handling and the use of catering premises.

Purchasing, Costing and Finance: covers financial aspects of running a catering business.

Available options, which vary from college to college, include:

Accommodation services	Front office operations
Financial control	Marketing
Food and drink operations	Modern languages
Food preparation	Tourism

The full-time courses include work experience and practical assignments, with a chance to practise the skills learned in college. National Certificate courses take two years part time and National Diploma courses take two years full time or three years part time and are available at more than 160 colleges.

3. *Higher National courses in Hotel, Catering and Institutional Management.* These lead to careers in accounting and finance, banquet and conference organising, catering companies, hospitals, hotels, personnel and training, residential homes and restaurants. Core subjects are:

Work Organisations: structure of organisations in the industry, and how they are run in a cost-effective way.

The External Environment: how hotel and catering organisations respond to external pressures, such as the economic, social and legal policies of local, central and international governments.

Operational Techniques and Procedures: develops skills needed to run a hotel and catering business efficiently, including the use of computers; the importance of customer care.

Physical Resource Management: the management and control of materials, equipment and property, including selection, purchasing, care and maintenance.

Human Resource Management: develops skills needed for effective manpower planning, including recruitment and training, and legal and financial matters relating to the employment of staff.

Available options include:

Accommodation management
Applied nutrition
Catering management
Catering technology
Conference and banqueting management
Financial management
Food and drink management
Gastronomy
Leisure resource management
Licensed trade management
Manpower studies and personnel administration
Modern languages
Property management
Public sector hotel services management
Purchasing and materials management
Sales and marketing
Small business enterprise
Tourism and hospitality management.

Over 30 colleges run the HNC and HND courses; the HNC course normally takes two years part time; HND takes two years full time or three years as a sandwich course. They provide at least 26 weeks' work experience, and include practical assignments. Assessment is by a range of methods including assignments, projects, case studies and practical exercises as well as examinations; an assignment might be a feasibility study and business plan for the purchase of a new restaurant, or the planning of a marketing strategy and campaign for a restaurant.

Both HNC and HND in Hotel and Catering can lead straight into the second year of a degree course in a related subject.

BTEC Continuing Education courses are for adults who want to update their skills. The Continuing Education Diploma in Hospitality Management is assessed through project work and not by examination.

Entry Qualifications

BTEC First Certificates and Diplomas. A student should have left school and be at least 16 years old. No formal examination passes are required, but a candidate will be expected to show evidence of an ability to benefit from the course.

BTEC National Certificates and Diplomas. A student should be at least 16 years old and normally needs a BTEC First Certificate or Diploma, or four GCSE grade C or above, or a suitable alternative qualification such as a CPVE.

BTEC Higher National Certificates and Diplomas: A student should normally be at least 18 years old and hold an appropriate BTEC National award or at least one A level and appropriate GCSEs at grade C or above. Colleges may also accept other qualifications or experience. Requirements depend on the individual course. Suitable A level subjects would be science or a related subject; students should also have GCSE passes in subjects testing literacy and numeracy.

BTEC Continuing Education Certificates, Diplomas and Units. A student should normally be at least 21, or have had at least three years' appropriate work experience. Entry qualifications vary between courses.

SCOTVEC

SCOTVEC (Scottish Vocational Education Council) offers a large number of individual modules at National Certificate and HNC/HND level. National Certificates in Food and Catering are available in modules of Hotel and Commercial Catering; Cooking and Food and Drink Preparation; Home Economics; Food Science and Food Manufacture and Distribution. They are offered at a range of approved centres including colleges, schools and private training organisations and can be taken on a full-time, part-time or open/distance learning basis.

There are 21 colleges validated to offer the HNC in Hospitality

Operations and 10 colleges validated to offer the HND in Hospitality Management. As the different colleges devise their own programmes of modules, it is necessary to approach the colleges themselves to find out what they offer.

SCOTVEC issues a Record of Education and Training (RET), which is a certificate that records the achievements in education and training of each person registered. New units, modules and qualifications are added to the RET as they are gained, even if there has been a gap of several years in training.

NVQ/SVQ (National/Scottish Vocational Qualifications). NVQ/SVQs, which are replacing Caterbase and City and Guilds qualifications, are based on workplace assessments. In the case of qualifications gained during a college course, the assessments are carried out either in conditions that closely match a workplace situation, such as a restaurant or kitchen, or during work experience or after starting work. These qualifications tie in with similar qualifications in the EC, and will be recognised throughout Europe.

NVQs and SVQs start from Level 1, semi-skilled, and go up to Level 5, which is senior management. In the hotel and catering industry they cover all types of skills, including cooking and serving food and drink, the work of a luggage porter or room attendant, housekeeping and catering management. Each NVQ/SVQ consists of several units of competence, recognised as a credit unit on the certificate. NVQ and SVQ titles are:

Level 1: Catering and Hospitality
 Reception and Portering
 Housekeeping
 Guest Service
 Serving Food and Drink – Bar
 Serving Food and Drink – Counter
 Serving Food and Drink – Table/Tray
 Food Preparation and Cooking – General
 Food Preparation and Cooking – Quick Service

Level 2: Catering and Hospitality
 Reception
 Serving Food and Drink – Restaurant
 Serving Food and Drink – Bar
 General
 Food Preparation and Cooking

Level 3: Catering and Hospitality Supervisory Management
Reception (three routes: (a) general; (b) functions; (c) portering)
Housekeeping
Food and Drink Service (three routes: (a) table; (b) counter; (c) drinks)
Food Preparation and Cooking
On-licensed premises Supervisory Management.

Level 4: Catering and Hospitality Management
Reception (two routes: (a) general; (b) functions)
Food and Drink Service (two routes: (a) food; (b) drinks)
Housekeeping
Food Preparation and Cooking
On-licensed Premises Management

BTEC (Business and Technology Education Council) is one organisation that awards NVQ/SVQs in the hotel and catering industry. Other award-making bodies in the industry are: The Scottish Vocational Education Council (SCOTVEC), The British Institute of Innkeeping (BII), City and Guilds of London Institute (C&G), Hotel Catering & Institutional Management Association (HCIMA) and the Hotel and Catering Training Company (HCTC). They approve companies offering NVQ/SVQs, register candidates, verify the work of assessors and issue the certificates.

NVQs are roughly equivalent to BTEC qualifications: NVQ Level 2 to BTEC First; NVQ Level 3 to BTEC National; NVQ Level 4 to BTEC Higher National and Continuing Education Certificate.

NVQs are offered by C&G at Levels 1 to 3; C&G plus HCIMA qualifications are equivalent to Level 4. HCTC NVQs are offered at Levels 1 to 4. HCTC and BII are offered at Levels 3 and 4 on-licensed premises.

SVQs are offered by HCTC and SCOTVEC at Levels 1 and 2. HCTC, SCOTVEC and HCIMA at Levels 3 and 4. HCTC, SCOTVEC and BII at Levels 3 and 4 on-licensed premises.

There are no entry requirements for NVQs and SVQs, or age restrictions. There are also no fixed timescales; a major feature of the qualifications is that they are taken when the candidate is ready, at his or her own pace. Entry can be at any level, through colleges, employers or other providers of training, with full credit given for previous experience and qualifications.

Degree Courses
Degree courses in Hotel and Catering Management are offered at

universities and other colleges. Degree courses require at least two A levels or H grades; two AS levels are considered equivalent to one A level. Special subject requirements for GCSE passes are English, another European language, mathematics and a science subject. It is advisable to have had some work experience in the catering industry before applying for admission to a degree course. Four-year courses include a year's practical experience, which could give an opportunity for a placement abroad. There are also one-year postgraduate courses for those who have a degree in a subject not directly related to hotel management; these lead to the Postgraduate Diploma in Hotel and Catering Administration.

Holders of non-catering degrees can also take the HCIMA (Hotel Catering & Institutional Management Association) Professional Qualification *Exceptional Entry* at one-year full-time intensive college-based courses which include a short period of work experience. The award of the HCIMA's Certificate allows entry to Intermediate membership of the HCIMA, leading to Licentiateship of the Association and eventual full membership. Further details of colleges offering graduate-entry courses are given in Chapter 11.

Case Study
Keith is a Surrey University undergraduate in his second year of a four-year BSc Honours course in hotel and catering management. He is doing his one year's practical in a 42-bedroom hotel in a country town.

> I was at a grammar school in Newcastle and after passing A levels in geography, economics and mathematics I decided to go into the hotel business. My mother is a domestic science teacher so I was introduced to catering from an early age. I was offered places at both Strathclyde and Surrey, but decided on the latter.
>
> Surrey has an intake of 64 students, 32 girls and 32 boys, all of whom have to find suitable places for their one year's practical. During the year out everyone earns around £120 a week and is treated as a normal member of staff.
>
> I have been working in the reception office together with a girl receptionist, booking in newcomers, handling keys, cheques and incoming telephone calls. Next week I am moving to the still room. I had to write two reports for the exams. The first was on institutional catering and the second on kosher catering. I found some useful information on the latter at the Kosher Centre in London. I also found the university library which contained a Cornell University report on institutional catering very helpful, as so many of the textbooks are

quickly out of date. I have already taken two exams and have one more left. My course tutor at Surrey visits me, and the degree is awarded on continuous assessment as well as exam results.

I like the work and hope to end up in a medium-sized hotel similar to the one I am working in at the moment. The hours suit me quite well, either 7.30 am to 3.30 pm or late shift 3.30 pm to 11.30 pm, but I think that they might not be so convenient if I was married and living some way from my work. To make extra money I work in the bar at night and find it a good way to meet people. Going back to Surrey will be strange, but I have learnt a lot here.

Restaurant Manager

The restaurant manager may be an assistant manager of the hotel or, in some rare cases, the restaurant is run as a separate establishment from the hotel itself, with its own opening hours, social events, booking arrangements for tables, and tariffs. A good knowledge of food and drink, staff relations, finance and stock control, and an ability to get on well with people are essential requirements.

A restaurant manager plans menus and is in charge of ordering the food, so profits will depend on skills in buying fresh foods at the right price. Menus are planned in consultation with the chef, and the manager is also responsible for ordering bar stocks. As hotel restaurants are open not only for dinner but also at breakfast and lunch-time, shifts for waiting and bar staff have to be planned throughout the day and the restaurant manager must take unsocial hours into account, allowing staff their quotas of off-duty periods. The manager will normally work during the busiest times of the day. Many of the jobs are residential, with food provided.

Training

Restaurant managers may have BTEC/SCOTVEC qualifications or have NVQ/SVQ Level 3 or Level 4 qualifications in Catering and Hospitality Supervisory Management. Restaurant managers in hotel groups may have a degree, BTEC Higher National Diploma or a professional qualification from the HCIMA, and would be able to move into general management within the group. School-leavers need four GCSE passes before taking a BTEC or HCIMA course.

Chef

The *chef de cuisine* or head chef commands a great deal of

respect, status, and a high salary. He will be well qualified, and as well as practical skills he must have experience in staff management because under him are a number of specialist chefs who have to be organised as a team. In a large hotel, the terminology in the kitchen is in French and the following assistant chefs are employed:

Sous-chef - the under chef or deputy chef
Chefs de Partie - the heads of sections. A large hotel usually has six sections, each with a *chef de partie*. These are known as:

Chef Gardemanger - the chef in charge of the larder
Chef Entremetier - the vegetable chef
Chef Rôtisseur - the roasting chef
Chef Poissonier - the fish chef
Chef Saucier - the entrée chef
Chef Pâtissier - the chef in charge of sweets, cakes etc.

There may also be a *chef potager*, or soup and garnish chef, and a *chef tournant*, who will step in and take charge of any action during illness or holiday periods.

Menus are planned by the head chef, who reports direct to the hotel manager every day to discuss the ordering of food, staff arrangements in the kitchen, rotas and shift systems, and the progress of the *commis-chefs*. These are apprentice chefs, usually on a three-year apprenticeship including day release classes at the local technical college. Here they take a City and Guilds 706 catering course and do prctical training with each of the *chefs de partie* in turn. Training can take up to five years. Apprentices in small restaurants often take the same course and most school leavers who want a career in hotel catering start as a trainee chef; many of the trainees have also moved into catering from YT courses.

Many young people entering go to a college to study for the NVQ and other courses (see Chapter 12), join a firm offering training on the job (see Chapter 10) or, for management, take a degree course, or the two-year BTEC HND hotel and catering management course and then, after obtaining some practical experience, begin to make progress in their career.

Case Study
Tracey is just 17 and is a *trainee chef*. She is studying for her City and Guilds 706 exams on a three-year day-release course at the

local technical college, 25 miles from where she works. The restaurant owner is a qualified trainer and gets a grant from the board for Tracey and her fellow trainee chef.

I earn about £130 a week but there is overtime and all staff in the restaurant get a share of the tips, whether or not they come into contact with the public. I work a rota, either 9 am to 4pm or 3.15 to 11.00 pm. I work six days a week and whenever I change rota I have a rest day off. One bonus is that the sea is a few hundred yards from the restaurant so I can lie on the beach and sunbathe, when I have the chance.

Meals are free for all staff and, if the restaurant is not busy, we use a small front room. The kitchen itself is small, very well equipped, and has an electric fan and extractor. I cook on an electric stove and, as omelettes are a favourite with the customers, there are three or four trays of eggs ready for adding to the frying pan. Sometimes the chip pan has been known to catch fire and there is a special blanket used for putting it out. Safety and hygiene are vital parts of the course.

I like my Wednesdays at college. I am never sure what we will be asked to cook. During the first part of the morning we have theory and at midday we are given our practical for the afternoon. It could be some sort of meat dish or a complicated sweet. I'm afraid that my mayonnaise curdled; it was the only one of the class that did, but the family still enjoyed it. I take my college dishes back home in a special basket in the bus.

My employer and his wife both work in the restaurant, where they specialise in fast food. They do not have many tables and it pays to get customers in and out in half an hour if possible. Although I'm not cooking very exotic dishes, I will end up with a useful qualification that will allow me to work in any part of the country.

Head Barman

The control and supervision of the bar, stocks of wine, beer and spirits is the job of the head barman or bar manager. His staff will usually include a barmaid or barman who is responsible for serving drinks, taking the money, occasionally working as a wine waiter, cleaning shelves, glasses and the bar itself. The head barman is in charge of bar equipment, hygiene and security, and usually has a head cellarman and a cellarman under his control. They work in the cellars, look after, and keep a stock control of the wine. The wine is ordered by the wine waiter, or *sommelier*, who is responsible to the head waiter.

Bar staff do not need any special qualifications except an ability for mental arithmetic, and must be over 18 before they can serve alcoholic drinks. There are NVQs in Levels 1 and 2 covering beverage service, and at Level 3, on Licensed Premises Supervisory. Information on colleges offering courses in bar and alcoholic beverage services is given in 'A Guide to Hotel and Catering Courses', from the Hotel and Training Catering Company.

Head Waiter

The head waiter in any hotel is an important person. Like the head barman, he is often an older man with several years' experience behind him. He is responsible for allocation of tables, and is in charge of other waiters or waitresses; if the restaurant offers *haute cuisine* and provides a silver service, he has to see his waiters or *chefs de rang* are qualified to serve main meals at tables from silver dishes, using a fork and spoon. He instructs the apprentice waiters, occasionally presents the bill, provides a trolley service – this involves *gueridon* or *flambé* service – and, if necessary, serves meals to guests in rooms, though this is more usually done by floor waiters.

The *chef de rang* looks after a group of tables and the *commis de rang* assists with serving vegetables and side dishes. The *commis*, or assistant, usually brings in the food from the kitchen and helps with clearing up.

The restaurant sometimes has a cocktail barman and a wine waiter. The latter is responsible for collecting orders for wine and other beverages, advising on their selection, deputising for the head waiter, collecting and preparing his own accounts, and ensuring that the cellarman takes proper care of his wines.

Non-Catering Occupations in a Large Hotel

Head Receptionist

This is an important position as the head receptionist is the first to welcome the guests. Bookings are acknowledged, the room chart kept up to date, keys and rooms allocated, and accounts for guests (restaurant, bar, newspapers, telephone calls etc) are collated and charged. Nowadays, knowledge of and ability to use office machinery such as word processors and personal computers is an advantage. The head receptionist is responsible for the other receptionists, who often work on a rota basis, and for the enquiry clerk, cashier and switchboard operator. Because of the evening and weekend shift work, receptionists often live in. Receptionists may take NVQs in Reception at Levels 1, 2, 3 and 4.

Head Porter

The head porter is responsible for other porters and cloakroom staff and for organising day and night shifts, and must be prepared to deal with any emergency, eg fire. The hall porter carries luggage to rooms, parks cars, cleans the foyer and orders taxis. The night porter may book in late arrivals, serve snacks and beverages, order newspapers, and prepare and serve early breakfasts and morning teas. Porters usually wear uniform (and sometimes trainee managers do the job as part of their training).

Housekeeper

The housekeeper is in charge of the servicing of the guests' accommodation. She supervises the chambermaids, room maids, cleaners, seamstresses, and other floor staff apart from waiters. In addition she is responsible for the stores, maintenance, laundry and flower arrangements. Some housekeepers live in the hotel. It is possible to train as a housekeeper by taking NVQs in Catering and Hospitality, Housekeeping, Levels 1, 3 and 4. There is a BTEC First Certificate/Diploma in Hotel and Catering Studies (Hotel Reception) and BTEC National Certificate/Diploma in Hotel, Catering and Institutional Operations (Housekeeping). SCOTVEC programmes in hotel, catering and institutional subjects are also suitable for housekeepers (see Chapter 12). Although staff numbers have been cut back in some hotel jobs, this is an area in which job prospects have improved. There can be opportunities in hotel chains for housekeepers to move into hotel, catering or conference organisation management.

Room Attendant

The bedrooms and public rooms in a hotel are cleaned by the room attendants or chambermaids, often working in pairs. In the bedrooms, this includes cleaning the bathroom and re-supplying with clean towels and soaps, changing the sheets, emptying the rubbish bin and leaving the room tidy; work starts as soon as the room is left empty by the guests. The room attendant may take early morning tea and papers to the room as well. The public rooms and corridors are cleaned first, while the guests are still in their rooms. Other jobs, such as washing walls, may be tackled after the routine cleaning is finished. Hours may be from 7.30 am to 3.30 pm and the work is often part-time or seasonal, especially in the tourist related holiday centres. There are good opportunities for promotion to supervisory level. Room attendants can take NVQ units of competence in skills including the preparing of beds for customer use as part of Housekeeping, Level 1. NVQs are usually undertaken as part of a hotel's training scheme.

Kitchen Assistant

A kitchen assistant is responsible for keeping the kitchen clean, including tiles, floors, work areas and cooking utensils while food is being prepared, and stacking the dishwashers with china, glasses and cutlery when it is being served by the waiting staff. Kitchen assistants also help in the preparation of food, preparing vegetables, cleaning and scaling fresh fish, boning meat and cutting it into joints, weighing ingredients ready for baking or perhaps making green salads. No specific qualifications are required and assistants will be trained on the job with the chance of training to become a cook or chef. Prospects in this area of work are good, both in hotel work and with food processinag companies.

Kitchen Porter

The kitchen porter stores the incoming goods, such as sacks of vegetables or sides of meat, in the store room and larder ready for the kitchen staff and notifies the chef if supplies are running low. He also disposes of all the rubbish and runs occasional errands.

Catering Manager

Large hotel chains may employ a catering manager to take charge of special events such as a wedding reception or charity ball. The manager will plan the events and make sure that everything is 'all right on the night'. Organisation is the main aspect of the work, covering every detail from flowers, numbers of glasses (allowing for breakages) and plates, to the provision of food.

A catering manager may work at head office, supervising regional managers, arranging the purchase of pre-cooked food, if necessary, and dealing with suppliers. Catering managers also work for contract catering companies or on a self-employed basis; they may work in the tourist and leisure industry or supply catering services to institutions. Training will be similar to a hotel manager's, with NVQ, BTEC or SCOTVEC or HCIMA qualifications and possible promotion to head office in large companies.

Conference and Banqueting Manager

A newly expanding part of a hotel's business is concerned with providing facilities for business bookings, conferences and special functions. Large hotel groups have their own conference departments with conference service managers who act as liaison officers between the venue and the client. The conference manager may have to organise Telex, Prestel and secretarial facilities as well as food and accommodation, and the hotel would provide audio-visual equipment, a screen and amplification to be used for presentations and promotions. There may also be excursions to organise, and at the end of the day the whole event would be costed and invoiced by the conference manager. Special functions such as banquets would involve menus, rooms, music facilities, private bars and floral decorations. Conference managers are also employed by large businesses who hold many meetings and courses each year, by professional associations, convention centres, local government and independent agencies.

There are no established qualifications as conference organising is a relatively new profession. Conference organisers usually have a university degree or BTEC business studies or hotel, catering and institutional management qualifications, and experience in business or in the leisure industry.

Banqueting Staff

Hotels that have a banqueting room usually employ part-time staff specially for the occasion. Flower arrangers will be subcontracted; the meal will be plate service.

Catering Staff in Medium and Small Hotels

Cooks

Most cooks have trained for two years, and then worked as an assistant cook in a large kitchen, or as a senior cook in a small one.

In speciality restaurants, eg steak bars, training is often on the job; in cafeterias the meals are pre-cooked and kept warm, so that little training is required.

Restaurant Waiter

As in the case of a large hotel offering *haute cuisine*, the waiter or waitress must be trained to provide silver service. The main requirements of a successful waiter or waitress are an engaging manner, smart appearance, speed, a good memory and, above all, courtesy. Waiting staff usually receive tips direct or through a pooled system or via a service charge.

A Medium-Sized Hotel

Situation
The County Hotel is an old-fashioned building, built for the stagecoach era, but the visitor is soon aware that it has been converted to provide maximum comfort and amenities for its customers. The main reception desk is at the back of the hotel, adjacent to the car park. The front door leads straight into the Brendon Bar. This is very convenient for lunch-hour customers. There is a large banqueting room used for local conferences with access from the back. At Easter a successful stamp exhibition and fair were held here: the hotel staff were not involved as catering was not laid on, but the general manager organised the fair, as he is a keen stamp collector, and people came from as far away as France just to attend.

Staff
The County Hotel is a 68-bed hotel in a provincial town; it belongs to a well-known hotel group. It has 56 full-time staff, and a team of casual workers called in as required, for the buttery or for the banquets, as waiters and waitresses. Also on the staff chart are apprentice chefs, who are taking a day-release/NVQ course at the local technical college, and two young people on work experience supplied by the local careers office, who work in reception and as chambermaids. (Different schemes operate in conjunction with the schools up and down the country to provide work experience for young people. Careers offices are not necessarily involved; one scheme in Essex is called Project Trident.) All areas have deputies to allow for sickness and holidays so that each manager's job, including the general manager's, is covered.

In charge of all personnel work is the assistant manager, personnel training. Miss Anderson was a group trainee, who joined the firm after completing her HND course in hotel management in Glasgow. She tends to get moved on every two years in order to get experience of all aspects of hotel work. This can cause complications in getting to grips with the difficult job of sorting out staff training, wages with the support of the accountant, holidays etc. Although she keeps a close eye on all matters relating to staff, she is not personally responsible for the casual staff, function bar staff, and banqueting. There are short weekend courses provided. These are usually held at one of the group's own hotels; some of the subjects covered on these courses are new approaches to management and finance. The staff chart is shown overleaf.

A Small Hotel

Lionel Hebditch and Michael Mundy own the Rylstone Hotel in Dorset. Because of its size and the fact that it is licensed, they need outside help to run it efficiently. The amount of assistance they need naturally varies with the time of year and volume of business. The months between Easter and the last bank holiday break are usually the busiest for seaside hotels (also the Christmas and New Year break if open for trade). As Lionel Hebditch says:

> You need to wear many hats to be in this trade. I cut my catering teeth on a slightly smaller, leasehold property with 16 bedrooms and took to the business straight away. It seemed a natural progression to buy this larger, freehold hotel. We are placed in a good position for easy access to the sea, which is quite close by, and are only a short ride to the town, which offers a wide range of shops and entertainments.
>
> We take pride in the service and menu we offer, so rely on capable staff to help run our hotel efficiently and well. Every member of staff is as important as the next; when a link of the 'chain' is broken, things can quickly go awry! This is where the ability to be an all rounder comes in handy. When working at full capacity, we usually have two chambermaids, two waitresses and a dishwasher; my partner does the cooking. During the off season (or when it's quieter) we can cope quite well with only one or two staff.
>
> Staff are not difficult to come by – they are culled from catering colleges, careers offices, various schools (sometimes linked with the Youth Training scheme), foreign students (English language schools), Jobcentres, TECs and employment agencies. Some employees come recommended, or introduce themselves personally by an initial phone call or by coming along to the hotel. It is all a case of trial and error really; some people are more responsible and reliable than others.
>
> Catering colleges are usually excellent places from which to get staff, especially waiters/waitresses and cooks. And there are many opportunities for part-time work in the busy season (schools and colleges are closed for at least part of the summer). I personally look

for someone who is trustworthy, capable and reliable, neat in appearance and polite. And it goes without saying that common sense (which doesn't always go hand in hand with intelligence) is a valuable asset. It is a good feeling to be backed by capable staff; in fact it is the only way to run a truly successful business.

Running a Small Restaurant

We take as an example, a thriving, family-owned, restaurant known as Taylers, situated in the heart of a busy market town in Essex. It has an excellent reputation and caters for local residents and visitors alike, especially on market days – of which there are three. Their menu is realistically priced, and whether the call is for fish and chips, with all the frills, or something a little fancier, the public are given the very best value for money.

The manager – Glen Suters – attended a hotel school of catering and furthered his catering experience in Switzerland, Germany, South Africa, and the Far East.

It's a hectic life at times, particularly when we have a full house, but it's an interesting and varied one. Of course, there is much planning involved to ensure that customers' needs are properly catered for, and this includes anything from checking on the cleanliness and attractiveness of the surroundings to the quality and service of the food they are served. The job is many faceted, as one needs to have patience and understanding when dealing with staff problems, deliveries, customers' queries, paperwork and so on.

Lunch-time trade can be variable and one of the problems is the balancing of supply with demand. Evening and weekend bookings take out the guess work!

As to staff, we employ a dishwasher and kitchen porter, a *commis* waitress – an 18-year-old local girl at present studying for her City and Guilds second-year exams on a day-release course; five other waiters and waitresses (split between lunch and dinner duties) and a chef hailing from Yorkshire – ex Queens Moat and City of London work, government hospitality and Downing Street. We take on extra staff as and when the need arises, more particularly at weekends, or when catering for special functions and weddin.s.

I brought along my own chef; the young *commis* weaitress was supplied by the local Jobcentre, and the remaining staff were employed prior to my appointment. It goes without saying that the need for reliable staff is vital to the well being of both customer and restaurant.

We are able to offer a wide variety of English and European dishes, both at lunch-time and in the evening, to suit everyone's taste and pocket. Our *à la carte* menu is frequently changed to give free rein to

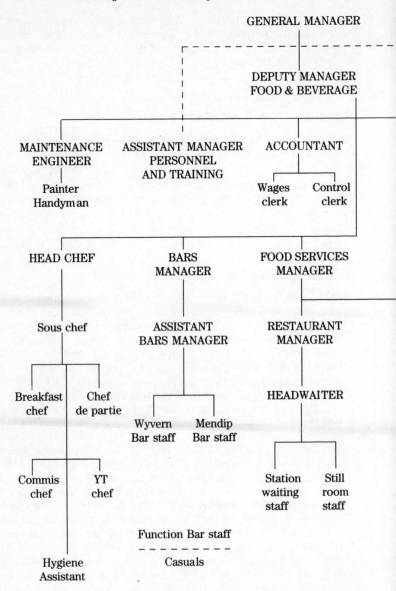

A staff chart for a medium-sized hotel

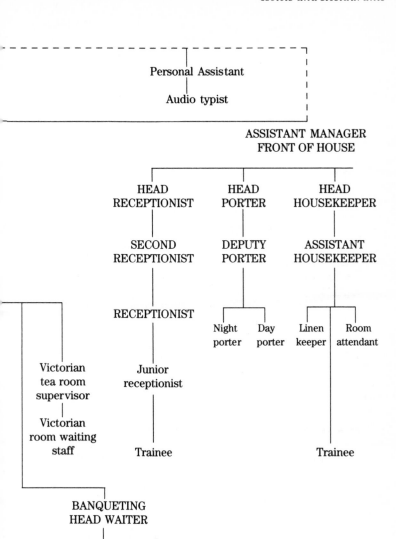

our chef's creative talents. Apart from a grill and steak menu, at lunch-time we offer a wide selection of home-made pies and puddings. Both menus are reasonably priced and include seasonal vegetables (there are no hidden extras to pay for). We also offer an interesting and well balanced wine list, and like to think that we given an efficient and friendly all-round service to the public.

Training

Training for non-management operational staff, both in catering and non-catering jobs, is provided through National Vocational Qualifications (NVQs) which are taking over from the City and Guilds qualifications, now being phased out. The NVQs are awarded through work-based assessment. Training and qualifications are offered by employers and other organisations approved by the Hotel and Catering Training Company. There are no pre-entry qualifications needed and awards are made through assessment at work, with units of competence being achieved as the trainee is ready for assessment, at his or her own pace. Certificates awarded by organisations such as City and Guilds and the Hotel Catering and Institutional Management Association cover qualifications in food preparation, food and beverage service, bar and alcoholic beverage service, front of house and accommodation operations (ie bedmaking, cleaning, and servicing swimming pools).

Salaries

Salaries vary throughout the country, with London and the south-east offering the highest. Average weekly salaries for live-out staff for 1991 were: Head chef, £257.04 (due to the recession this is lower than the 1990 average of £269.69); restaurant manager, £242.36; head receptionist £171.72; head housekeeper, £174.05; head porter, £161.32; room service waiter, £130.02; bar manager, £182.90.

Chapter 2
Contract and Institutional Catering

The world of institutional catering has been greatly altered in the last 25 years by the growth of contract catering. There are some very large organisations in the business in this country now that offer not only catering but also consultancy services, kitchen design, and vital information on aspects of hygiene and safety. It may be cheaper for a large firm or institution to hire a contract caterer than to employ its own catering staff.

As local and health authorities must now put contracts for school and hospital meal services out to tender, it is often independent contract caterers who win the contract. They also do the catering for independent schools, colleges, prisons, leisure centres, directors' dining rooms, the staff restaurant of offices and factories, snacks for shoppers in department stores and events such as Wimbledon and the Royal Windsor Horse Show.

There are now several large contract catering companies, such as Gardner Merchant, Compass, Sutcliffe Catering, Russell & Brand and Catering and Allied Staff.

Unlike most of the catering industry, contract catering offers relatively social hours, mainly Monday to Friday, without week-end work.

Job opportunities in catering companies include customer service assistants, waiting staff and kitchen assistants. There are careers opportunities for chefs, chef managers and catering managers, as well as for general group management. Training is given on the job, combined with off-job courses. These companies also have subsidiaries in other countries, within the EC and in America, the Far East and Australia.

Applicants are considered with City and Guilds and BTEC qualifications, or with a degree.

In 1991 the number of meals served by contract caterers was as below:

Sector	No of meals (millions)
Department stores	2.2
Construction sites	3.0
Training centres	8.1
Oil rigs	13.7
State education	30.2
Healthcare	38.2
Local authorities	41.0
Ministry of Defence	54.8
Catering for the public	60.0
Independent schools	81.4
Business and industry	322.0

Case Study

Richard is a contract catering manager in his thirties. He started his training in catering management on a two-year course at South Devon College, Torquay. He spent three years in industrial catering before joining a contract catering firm in Bristol. He started as a relief manager, but now has charge of a new contract, a large further education college, feeding some 800 staff and students per day in term time. He has a staff of 13 who were already on the education college staff (sometimes the caterer will supply the staff as well). His contract is fixed, so that he works to a budget. If his company victuals are for less than the budget then a percentage of this figure is returned to the customer. If his company steps over this figure then it pays the difference. The following diagram shows how he employs his staff.

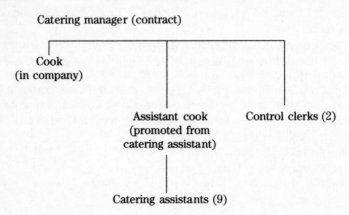

Catering manager (contract)

Cook
(in company)

Assistant cook
(promoted from
catering assistant)

Control clerks (2)

Catering assistants (9)

Every week I work out the menu with my cook. I have problems balancing the demand with ordering and wastage. The custom is variable; it may depend on the weather, transport problems, or on the popularity of a particular evening class.

I have recently been on a four-day training course organised by my firm's regional training manager in Bristol. I enjoy the work and receive four weeks' holiday in the summer. My staff are paid retainers so they come back in September, but the trend with both schools and colleges is to employ them for courses in the summer holidays. This means that there has to be someone on duty most of the time now; extra wages are paid during the holiday period. We have to maintain a high standard of catering or else the contract will not be renewed.

There are many firms of contract caterers, large and small, in the country. Some that provide training schemes for their staff are listed in Chapter 11.

It is important, however, that customers and young people choosing a firm realise that some contract caterers specialise in a particular type of catering, be it events, weddings, schools and colleges, factories, open-air or football stadiums. Some provide the equipment for hire only, and not the staff.

Function Caterers

An excellent example of a firmly established London-based family business - steadily gathering strength since 1933 - is now run by the third generation: Mr Dennis Chasney and his family.

We can boast five banqueting areas, and are able to offer rooms and suites for all occasions. For instance, our Windsor Room has a private bar area, is available until 6 pm and accommodates 16 guests for lunch, or for a small conference. The Stilton Room - on two levels - is ideal for a family party: 50 can be seated for a dinner, 60 for a buffet. There is a bar close by and an area for dancing. At the other end of the scale, our Cheshire Suite can comfortably seat 120 guests for a dinner dance, ideal for a large wedding party. Again, there is a separate bar, cloakroom and reception area.

When we are working flat out there is an enormous amount of organising involved, especially for wedding parties. Some couples leave most of the arrangements to us, including costings, flowers, printing, photographer and the hiring of a DJ etc. You have to be on your toes! The need for reliable staff can't be emphasised enough at such busy times, from kitchen hands to waiters and waitresses, cloakroom attendants to bar staff. Any disruption in the smooth running of the operation can put a lot of strain on other members of the team.

Apart from the usual attributes desirable in an employee, I would rate common sense high up on the list. It is easily as important as speed and efficiency. It is only natural that any employer offering a high-class service needs able, first-class assistants. The service given at a small luncheon gathering should be of the same high calibre as that given at the largest wedding party.

Our menu is extensive and varied. Banqueting menu suggestions range from ramekin of mackerel with mustard sauce, fillet of beef Wellington, a selection of vegetables, meringue glacé Chantilly (served with fresh cream, sauce or ice cream) with cheese and biscuits, coffee and mints, to 16 other menus. Special menus are offered for vegetarians, and other dietary needs are catered for. A comprehensive wine list is available, and our cellarman is always pleased to suggest appropriate wines, or to tell customers about the special wines in our cellar.

Being such a busy firm, we need to employ up to 50 staff when working at full capacity. Working hours vary a great deal because of the need for staff during the day when catering for business and private luncheons and meetings, as well as during the evening when we are heavily booked for functions and weddings.

Staff come from many sources: private advertising, personal introduction, Jobcentres, careers offices, employment agencies, catering colleges and schools.

School Meal Catering

In recent years, local education departments have made changes in school meal catering. The traditional three- or two-course meal, served hot to all staff and pupils, has been replaced by a cafeteria operation, where there is a choice of meals which are paid for on the spot. Many children take their own sandwiches. The contracts for supplying school meals go out to tender, and the LEA catering departments compete with independent caterers for the work. Most school meals are prepared on site in the school's kitchens, but some village schools still have meals cooked at a central kitchen some miles away and brought to them in a van.

In charge of the kitchen is the central kitchen supervisor. Cooks are usually on a weekly rota, and the blackboard is marked up with the meals required for the day. There are some general assistants who look after vegetable preparation, and early cooking is essential as most school meal vans set off at about 10.30 am. Special containers are used which have to be sterilised before they are packed and delivered. The driver has a meal at the last school on his delivery list, before returning with the containers which he collects, duly cleaned, on the reverse journey. The driver empties the swill and cleans the van, and the supervisor has to see that the paperwork has been completed and the kitchen cleaned before the next day's work begins.

Independent School Catering

Let us take for an example an independent school of about 600 boys and girls aged between 16 and 18; about one-third of these are day children and two-thirds are boarders. The catering manager has a strict budget to keep to, so that economy is a main consideration. He is keen to help young staff; and his four assistant cooks are all City and Guilds certificate holders on their first job. The kitchen structure is shown in the diagram below.

The catering manager works a rota with the deputy catering manager and two of the four cooks are always on duty. The other staff work a 40-hour week.

This school employs its own baker and butcher who work on a part-time basis as both own their own small businesses. This, however, is a fairly unusual arrangement.

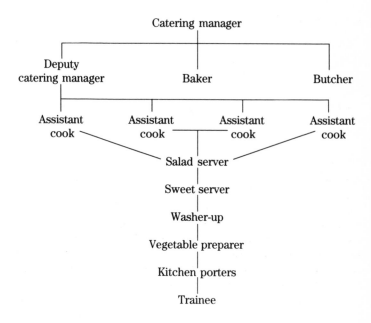

Case Study

Ben has had an unusual career before becoming a school catering officer in an independent school. He left school with a few O levels (GCSEs) including French, and was one of four British students at the Lausanne Hotel School. Lectures were all in French and Ben found the work very hard. He did placements at such famous restaurants as Maxims and the Palace Hotel Restaurant in Gstaad, before qualifying three years later.

On returning to London I worked as a receptionist/cashier at the Hyde Park Hotel in London. I was promoted after a year to assistant banqueting manager. This experience helped me to obtain the banqueting manager's job at the London Hilton at the age of 28. I spent some time there before moving to the same post at Quaglino's in Piccadilly. From there, after four years, I moved again to the position of food and beverage manager at the Royal Lancaster Hotel. By the early 1970s I was married with three children, and one day I forgot my son's first birthday. My wife said that I was absent from home so much that I didn't know my own children, so I decided to move.

I bought a small hotel on the fringe of Exmoor; with my wife, who had worked at the Mayfair Hotel, I spent ten years building up the hotel, which even today has a reputation for excellent cuisine. I sold it at the height of the property boom and took a long vacation. In April 1982 I decided it was time to get back to catering, but opportunities for work in West Somerset were limited. The advantage of schools is that they have long holidays, as well as reduced fees for your own children. I am now enjoying being a salaried member of staff once more.

Chapter 3
Forces Catering

All training for the catering arms of the services is carried out at the catering training centre at Aldershot in Hampshire, but each of the services operates its own catering school independently within the centre, with separate staff and facilities. Some of the staff, such as nutritionists, are civilians. During their training, catering staff and stewards are able to gain BTEC qualifications and NVQs equivalent to City and Guilds standards. At present the NVQs are in the process of being introduced; trainee recruits are able to have their work assessed during one-week placements with service units. Further training and qualifications are gained during their service career.

Army

The Army Catering Corps has its headquarters at Aldershot. It has the motto 'we sustain' and a badge of a flaming cauldron. Its members are to be found in every unit all over the world, from Northern Ireland to the South Atlantic. All cooks are trained as soldiers for an initial ten weeks at Aldershot, because in an emergency even the cook has to be able to fire a rifle.

Craft Training
All new entrants learn cookery which is taught by the most modern methods - closed circuit television is used on advanced courses - and they can gain NVQ qualifications and the Royal Institute or Public Health and Hygiene Certificate and Diploma. As well as cooking for large numbers, Army cooks have to know how to set up a field kitchen, which may have to be camouflaged and moved in a hurry. Promotion may be rapid and many A1 cooks, the highest craft qualification, are sergeants when still in their twenties. A1 cooks are regarded as holding qualifications equivalent to the advanced City and Guilds qualifications.

Promotion may be to warrant officer, in which position they may become instructors or they may command large kitchens.

Apprentice Chefs

Apprentice chefs join the Army between 15 years 9 months and 17 years 6 months. They receive a thorough two-year training in all aspects of cookery. They are treated as potential NCOs, and learn a soldier's skill as well as taking part in outside activities like climbing, sailing and orienteering. After two years they are posted to their unit, and when 18 can sign on for a minimum of three years as regular soldiers. The soldier with a craft is never short of work, and as a member of the Army Catering Corps many people depend on him.

For further information, contact your local Army Careers Information Office or Major D Sinclair ACC, Army Catering Corps, St Omer Barracks, Aldershot, Hants GV11 2BN; 0252 348091.

Royal Air Force

No formal educational qualifications are necessary for entry as a trades apprentice, although a GCSE/SCE in maths would be an advantage for those entering as catering clerks who deal with organisation and administration. The minimum age of entry for both chefs and catering clerks is 16 for men and 17 for women. It is necessary for all entrants to pass a short series of tests. Recruits take the standard six-week course at RAF Swinderby before going to the RAF School of Catering, Aldershot, for craft training. They spend about 12 weeks at Aldershot as leading aircraftmen before joining their unit which can be anywhere in the world.

Present day Harrier squadrons may be sited on small fields without proper runways, so the back-up troops, including cooks, have to be present there too. Most cooks are promoted to senior aircraftmen after 12 months' service, and after taking an education test can become corporals and sergeants when still in their twenties. Opportunities for further advancement occur, and many RAF cooks have reached a very high standard in their craft and won many catering competitions.

Civilian qualifications and experience in catering can qualify for entry at the rank of leading aircraftman or senior aircraftman, or for training as a commissioned catering officer.

Contact: Squadron Leader Bernie Chown, RAF Officers

Careers, London Road, Stanmore, Middx HA7 4PZ; 081-958 6377, ext 7163.

Royal Navy and Royal Marines

Navy Cooks

Royal Navy cooks have to be able to work to high standards. They may be required to cook for banquets on shore or for men at sea in a gale. Recruits spend seven weeks on preliminary training in HMS *Raleigh*, the New Entry shore training establishment at Torpoint in Cornwall, then go on to a 14-week course under the supervision of experienced instructors at the Royal Naval School of Cookery in Aldershot, where they learn skills including the preparation of stocks, soups and sauces, fish, meat and vegetable dishes, salads, desserts and baking. This is followed by a six-week professional course back at HMS *Raleigh* which covers catering for large numbers, management and accounting skills and computer techniques. Recruits then spend about 12 months in a shore galley before going to sea. Promotion is to leading cook; this means being qualified to City and Guilds 706/2 standard (NVQ Level 1). A cookery instructor is qualified by the standard of City and Guilds 706/3, and he may qualify for the Hotel and Catering Training Board's teaching certificate 730.

Stewards

Stewards, both men and women, act as waiters in shore establishments, and on board ship they serve food as well as drink in the wardroom. After basic training they spend six weeks in training at HMS *Raleigh*, learning the duties of wine steward, simple cookery and pantry work, wardroom organisation, as well as serving techniques. They may progress to leading steward (which indicates they are qualified to the standard of the City and Guilds 701/1, food service). A petty officer is regarded as having a qualification equivalent to the City and Guilds certificate 717, beverage service. Stewards can also gain professional qualifications, such as membership of the Cookery and Food Association. Training is followed by about nine months at a shore establishment before a sea appointment in a surface ship or submarine (women do not serve in submarines).

WREN Stewards

WREN stewards spend five weeks in initial training at HMS

Raleigh. This is followed by exactly the same training as male stewards in the art of serving food and drink, as well as looking after and organising accommodation. Promotion is similar to that for male stewards.

Royal Marines

Cooks with the Royal Marines have to do a full six months' commando training at the Commando Training Centre, Lympstone, to win their green beret, before going on to learn their professional skills on a seven-week course at the Royal Navy Cookery School at Aldershot. Successful completion of training can lead to a City and Guilds award. Chefs then return to Lympstone to learn how to cook in field conditions; cooking ranges from preparing meals in the main galley to preparing *haute cuisine* meals for formal dinners in the officers' mess. Entrants (aged 16 to 17½) must pass a selection test (reasoning, English language, numeracy and mechanical comprehension), interview, medical examination and Potential Recruits Course. There are annual tests for fitness and weapon skills, undertaken by all Royal Marines. Promotion prospects are excellent and there are opportunities to gain top civilian cookery qualifications.

Contact: Directorate of Fleet Supply, Ministry of Defence (Navy), Room 829, Empress State Building, London SW6 1TR; 071-385 1244.

Chapter 4

Transport and Hospital Catering

Transport Catering

Airports

Providing food for aeroplane flights is a highly specialised form of catering. Every year each airline meets with its catering company to calculate the budget and the type of meal for each journey. Some aircraft can carry cold meals only. Outward meals are stored by the handlers in the galley, and return meals in the hold. Every week the airline supplies details of the following week's flights; the actual passenger figures are not known until the day before. The duty officer at the airport supervises the loading, and keeps in touch with the production room where the caterers pack the meals. There is a production controller, who orders supplies for every meal – the crew tends to be fussier than the passengers – and the packing takes place at speed. The hand slice has to be set to produce exactly the right size of a slice of meat, and all apples etc are graded. Hygiene is very important, and an inspector sample-checks the food to see that everything is up to standard.

Some airport catering companies are required to dress the aircraft completely, which means putting magazines, bags etc in each seat, and checking dry stores such as toilet paper and soap. Nowadays the catering trucks have a special X-lift that raises them to the right height for the aircraft door from the lorry so that unloading can be done at cabin floor level. Drinks are usually served from pre-packed bars that are loaded in boxes on to the aircraft.

Merchant Marine Catering

For details of merchant marine catering opportunities contact: The Merchant Navy Training Board, 2–5 Minories, London EC3N 1BJ; tel: 071-283 2922. Catering staff are given training by their employers at the Merchant Navy's Catering College in Gravesend, Kent.

Police Catering

Qualified catering staff interested in catering for the 200 police establishments in London should contact: Catering Department, Metropolitan Police, Wellington House, 67 Buckingham Gate, London SW1E 6BE.

Hospital Catering

Hospital catering services provide food to thousands of patients, staff and visitors every day. The food is served as plated meals or bulk meals, and in cafeterias and restaurants. The catering premises, often using new food systems and the latest technology, use conventional cooking, cook-chill or cook-freeze, call-order or à la carte methods.

Hospital caterers must now make full use of their facilities; in addition to supplying meals to patients and staff, many also offer services to outside clients with fast-food bars, licensed restaurants and functions rooms. Competing with contract caterers, they can provide food for school meals services, and do the catering for wedding receptions and other functions.

Vacancies are often advertised in the local paper by health authorities and in *The Health Service Journal*. Newly qualified college leavers should also apply direct to hospitals.

Management

Within the NHS, the development of the General Hotel Services Department groups housekeeping services, reception and communication services in one management unit. Career opportunities exist at every level within housekeeping services, with progression through to supervisory and management level.

Supervisory staff should hold National Examination Board for Supervisory Staff or City and Guilds qualifications. Managers should hold a degree, BTEC HND or equivalent HCIMA.

The Hospital Caterers Association produces *The Hospital Caterers Association Journal*, and a careers guide which includes information on catering, housekeeping services, reception and communication services. Details from: Mrs M Bates FHCIMA, Hon. National Secretary, Craigavon Area Hospital, 68 Lurgan Road, Portadown BT63 5QQ; Portadown 334444.

Catering managers are in charge of large hospital catering departments. They plan menus, order supplies and are in charge of the day-to-day food preparation and service. They must be good committee members as their work brings them into contact with hospital management. They are aided by assistant catering managers.

Catering Supervisors take charge of small, individual units within a hospital.

Most new entrants to catering management hold the BTEC diploma or higher diploma in hotel catering and institutional management.

Cookery

Hospital kitchens are supervised by kitchen superintendents, normally mature people with all-round experience as cooks, and with previous hospital and staff management experience. They are responsible to the catering manager, and are in charge of the assistant cooks, skilled cooks and assistant head cooks. Most kitchens have a head cook who has passed the City and Guilds 706/1 exam, and assistant head cooks and above should hold the 706/2 qualification.

Training

Training and development opportunities include pofessional qualification, management and supervisory development, craft and trainer skills, customer care programmes, health and safety, first aid and food hygiene. Courses are run within hospitals or local colleges and training organisations, leading to qualifications such as Basic Food Hygiene and NVQs.

Many regional health authorities operate training schemes within the NHS Hotel Services Training Unit. Contact the nearest regional health authority office for further information. The Hotel Services Training Unit, which offers training and development in many areas for supervisory and management staff, can be contacted at: David Salomans House, Broomhill Road, Southborough, Tunbridge Wells, Kent TN3 0TG; 0892 515152.

Dining Room Staff

Dining room supervisors organise staff restaurants and take on and train dining room staff. The senior supervisor is in charge of all hospital food service areas.

The following chart illustrates a typical career path through the Hotel Services Management Development Programme.

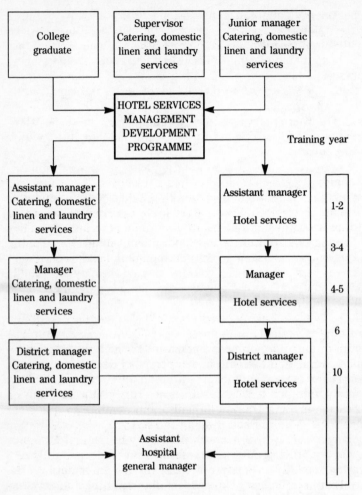

Chapter 5
Fast Food Catering

The pace of modern life has created a revolution in the fast food catering organisations. A good explanation of the industry is given by Peter Bertram in *Fast Food Operations*, where he divides the different kinds of fast food catering into eight categories: restaurants, cafeterias, buffets, coffee shops, public houses, take-away shops, event catering and mobile catering.

Restaurants

The hotel restaurant and *haute cuisine* restaurant are discussed in Chapter 1. Restaurants with specialised menus, a fast turnover of customers, and employing maximum use of convenience and frozen foods are best sited in high streets or near offices and factories.

Such fast food restaurants include grills, pizza houses, fried chicken, burger and steak bars, fish and chip shops and other specialised food establishments. Staff have to work quickly and look smart. They may have to do the frying, or add fillings to jacket potatoes, or cook vegetables. Shifts could be as early as 6 am for breakfast, or ending at midnight. Some employers offer free hairdressing, manicures, dental and medical treatment, as well as free uniforms and laundry.

Cafeterias

Self-service cafeterias are found in motorway service areas, department stores, schools, colleges and other establishments. Usually they have call-order bars where light meals can be cooked, and microwave ovens or bain-maries - vessels for cooking or heating food, placed in another vessel containing water, standing on a hot plate behind glass screens for hygienic reasons and so that the food looks attractive. The staff required are chefs, bain-marie attendants or counter hands, and a cashier.

No special qualifications are needed by staff in fast food shops, although there may be a test in mental arithmetic for those who will be adding up bills for customers and giving change. There is a City and Guilds specific skills scheme for call-order cooks, who learn about deep and shallow frying, grilling and boiling foods, and how to use catering equipment and tools. There is also a scheme for food service assistants, who learn basic food preparation, serving and table clearing. Work may be seasonal and first jobs are normally easy to obtain; promotion is possible in some fast food chains, though training would be needed.

Snack Bars

Snack bars and sandwich bars are similar to cafeterias but have no barrier rail to channel customers. They are found in theatres, railway stations etc. They occupy less space than cafeterias, provide a slower service, but require less staff. The attendant provides each customer with the food required, and may take the money for it as well if the food is packaged. Otherwise, for reasons of hygiene, a cashier should be employed too.

Coffee Shops

American-style coffee shops are found in many large hotels. They usually have stools or pew-style seating and serve coffee, snacks and light meals, some operating 24 hours a day. They should not be confused with the espresso coffee houses or the British tea shops, which serve a different clientèle. Many coffee shops have universal menus so that people can eat what they like when they like. It is now customary in many hotels for breakfast to be served in the coffee shop rather than the restaurant.

Public Houses

To make a profit, pubs need to offer food as well as drink. Pubs owned by breweries are either run by managers on behalf of the brewery, or let to tenants. A manager is paid a salary and possibly receives a bonus or takes part in a profit-sharing scheme. A tenant rents a public house from the brewery or other owner on agreed terms; he keeps the profits made from the trade he creates, and is also responsible for the outgoings. Free houses are free from any brewery tie; they are usually run by the owner, or a manager on his behalf. Staff employed are full- or part-time barmen or barmaids and cellar staff and, if there is a separate restaurant, waiters, waitresses and cooks. Pubs are currently the fastest-growing sector of the food market.

Training Schemes
Brewery companies run training courses for new managers and potential tenants, ranging from short courses of two weeks to courses lasting several months. Courses are also run by the Hotel and Catering Training Company and by further education colleges that offer full- or part-time courses in licensed house management. Courses lead to the qualifying examination of the British Institute of Innkeeping (BII).

Many colleges also offer courses and options at diploma and degree level designed for students who intend to specialise in the licensed trade.

Training courses leading to BII examinations are listed in *The Innkeepers Training Directory*, available from Morning Advertiser, Elvian House, Nixey Close, Slough, Berks SL1 1NQ (£5.95).

Take-Away Shops

The commonest take-away shop is the fish and chip bar. This is usually open in the evenings only until quite late at night, and sometimes staff include the manager/owner, and two or three part-time assistants. Other shops include: Chinese, Greek and Indian take-aways, where meals can be ordered in advance by a number system or by stating requirements over the counter, and can be carried home in foil containers, hot-food shops for office workers in cities, pizza houses, potato parlours, pancake houses and sandwich or hamburger bars. Staff employed are counter assistants as no washing-up or waiting is required, and very little preparation.

Event Catering

Most event organisers contract their catering out to contract caterers or, in the case of race tracks or stadiums owned by a city, the civic catering department will do the catering. Sometimes more than one caterer will attend a special show and there is always room for the individual operator, such as the hot dog stand holder, hot chestnut, hamburger or jacket potato vendors.

Mobile Catering

For years we have become accustomed to the ice cream van ringing its bell in the neighbourhood, and there are numerous mobile catering vans that attend race meetings, football matches, agricultural shows, and other outside events. Most are owner operated and tend to stay in one area, though some trade in the city during the winter and move to a seaside resort during the summer season.

Chapter 6
The Role of the Institutions and the HCTC

British Hospitality Association

Formerly the British Hotels and Restaurants' Association, the BHA has over 14,000 members and represents all kinds of establishments in the hotel and catering sector. It provides advice to members on all aspects of the industry, publishes an annual guide, *Hotels and Restaurants of Britain*, and the magazine *Voice*. It has a national council and nine divisional committees elected by members in the counties. Its special purpose committees include: a motorway service area operators' committee, a personnel and training committee, and an equipment and supplies committee. The Association has the facility of student exchange and overseas employment, and has overseas membership.

Further information can be obtained from: The British Hospitality Association, 40 Duke Street, London W1M 6HR.

The BHA is involved in a training scheme, the Hotel and Restaurant Trainee Placement Scheme which came into effect in 1988. The scheme places hotel and restaurant trainees throughout the European Community with hotels and restaurants approved as training centres. The training is mainly practical, and enables the trainee to acquire foreign language skills. Training lasts six months to a year during which most positions will be covered: kitchen, service, reception, administration and management. At the end of the period the trainee will receive an official Hotel and Restaurant Industry in the European Community (HOTREC)/EC certificate. Candidates must be over 18 and have successfully completed an initial training course in a hotel school, training centre or hotel or restaurant in an EC country.

The Catering Teachers' Association

Founded in 1960, the CTA is a teachers' association and holds regular meetings to discuss new courses and revisions to existing courses. It publishes a newsletter and runs courses at both national and regional level. For further details contact: Peter Gamble, CTA, c/o High Peak College, Harpur Hill, Buxton, Derbyshire SK17 9JZ; 0298 71100.

The City and Guilds of London Institute

Most young people entering technical college to pursue catering, hotel reception or similar careers, now study for certificates issued by the City and Guilds of London Institute. For information on NVQs, see page 17.

City and Guilds awards are at several levels – pre-vocational, occupational (three levels), career extension (either occupational or general) obtained through successful performance in tests or other assessments, and senior professional, Licentiate-ship (LCGI), Graduateship (CGLI), Associateship (ACGLI), Membership (MCGI) and Fellowship (FCGI).

Hotels and catering awards offered by C&G are:

Cookery Certificates (3320), C&G Levels 2 and 3. The Cookery Certificate is designed to stimulate an interest in cookery; the Cook's Professional Certificate aims to develop a high standard of advanced cookery skills.

Preliminary Cookery (3330), C&G Level 1. For students with special needs.

Fish frying, NVQ at Levels 1 and 2. For people working in fried fish retail outlets.

General Catering (7050), C&G Level 1. A general introductory course to professional catering.

Cookery for the Catering Industry (7060), C&G Levels 1, 2 and 3. The scheme aims to provide candidates with the skills and knowledge for preparing and cooking food in hotels, restaurants and other catering establishments. Part III allows candidates to specialise in either the kitchen and larder, pastry or advanced pastry sectors.

Food and Beverage Service (7070), C&G Levels 1 and 2. Qualifies in practical skills, including communication and presentation skills as well as serving and clearing foods in various types of service. Part II includes supervision, cost control, legislation and industrial relations.

Accommodation Services (7080), C&G Level 2. For prospective housekeepers in hotels, clubs and similar residential establishments, including hospitals.

Patisserie (7110), C&G Level 2. Usually offered with Cookery and Skills for the Catering Industry (7060-2).

Beverage Sales and Service (7170), C&G Level 2. Includes interpersonal skills.

Diploma in Reception and Front Office Practice (7200), C&G Level 2. Skills in practical reception plus current technology.

NVQ in Catering and Hospitality Level 1 (7241). Introductory qualification covering food preparation and service, housekeeping and reception.

NVQ in Catering and Hospitality Level 2 (7242). Covers food service and preparation, and reception.

NVQ in Catering and Hospitality Supervisory Management Level 3 (7243).

NVQ in Catering and Hospitality – On Licensed Premises Supervisory Management Level 3 (7243-05).

NVQ in Catering and Hospitality Management Level 4 (7244). Awarded jointly with HCIMA and aimed at candidates in managerial positions in the food preparation and cooking, reception, housekeeping and food and drink service sectors.

NVQ in Catering and Hospitality – On Licensed Premises Management Level 4 (7244-05).

For further details of CGLI courses contact: Division 21, 46 Britannia Street, London WC1X 9RG.

The Cookery and Food Association

The earliest of the existing culinary associations, the CFA assists with the education both of chefs and of young people in cookery, and honours those who distinguish themselves in the promotion of cookery. The Craft Guild of Chefs and the Restaurant Services Guild forms part of the CFA, and encourages chefs to reach a high standard of craftsmanship.

For juniors, there is a junior membership open to catering students and trainees. After a year of training in industry and with the possession of the City and Guilds 706/1 or equivalent qualification, juniors can become craftsmen II. The craftsman I is awarded to those who have been working in a kitchen for at least four to five years. The CFA organises the annual Hotelympia exhibition, and publishes a magazine entitled *Food and Cookery Review* which appears bi-monthly. Further information can be obtained from: The Cookery and Food Association, 1 Victoria Parade, by 331 Sandycombe Road, Richmond, Surrey TW9 3NB.

The Hotel & Catering Training Company

The HCTC's Training Division provides commercial training services and support materials for the hotel, catering, tourism and leisure industries. There are over 60 training centres throughout the UK, offering youth and adult training programmes; these are business and operational management training for supervisors, junior and middle managers, trainer training and support for NVQs and SVQs.

Short training courses are provided in a variety of subjects, including health and safety, following the Food Safety Act 1990 which introduced tight new regulations governing the handling and serving of food. There is also a Hygiene Instructor course, the Royal Environmental Health Institute of Scotland's Elementary Food Hygiene course and the REHIS Intermediate Food Hygiene course.

Other short courses offered by the HCTC are Operational Management, Business Management, Assessor and Verifier training programmes, Trainer training and Craft training. The HCTC also has a catalogue of videos, books, training aids, self-study units and research reports to support on- and off-the-job training, college courses, distance learning and private study.

Further information from the Training Division's regional offices:

Southern Region: International House, High Street, Ealing, London W5 5DB; 081-579 2400

Central Region: Second Floor, Stonebow House, The Stonebow, York YO1 2NP; 0904 626134

Western Region: Prudential Buildings, Wine Street, Bristol BS1 2PH; 0272 264074

Scotland and Northern Ireland: Capital House, 9 Logie Mill, Edinburgh EH7 4HG; 031-557 4677.

The Hotel Catering & Institutional Management Association

Established in 1971 when the Hotel & Catering Institute merged with the Institutional Management Association, the HCIMA has three main aims:

1. to set up and maintain standards;
2. to win greater recognition for professional managers in all parts of the industry;
3. to help managers and potential managers develop and maintain their knowledge and abilities.

The HCIMA runs professional qualification courses, and assists with management development, in-house training and career counselling.

There are six grades of membership from student to fellow. Student members must be studying for one of the HCIMA-approved qualifications. To become a fellow, it is necessary to have held a position of responsibility in the industry for at least five years or have written an acceptable thesis; or have been a corporate member for ten years or an associate member for four years; or have been outstandingly successful in the profession.

Examinations
The HCIMA offers two qualifications. The Professional Certificate is for those aspiring to, or working at, supervisory level; the Professional Diploma is for supervisors and first-line managers who aspire to more senior levels of management. Applications for HCIMA programmes are made through colleges.

Professional Certificate: study is through part-time or block-release college courses over two years. Entry requirements: candidates must either be working in appropriate employment or must have at least two years' full-time employment in the industry, including some experience at supervisory level. Further qualifications are: (a) three years' appropriate employment and one year's full-time or two years' part-time course, eg BTEC First Certificate or Diploma or SCOTVEC National Certificate modules in Hotel and Catering; or successful completion of a catering YT programme or holding an appropriate CGLI certificate, or (b) other combinations of hotel and catering craft or supervisory qualifications and experience, or (c) appropriate work experience and four GCSEs grades A to C, or equivalent, in subjects demonstrating command of English language, literacy, numeracy and science.

Professional Diploma: Study is through a one-year full-time or two-year sandwich programme, or a three-year day-release course. Candidates must either be working in appropriate employment with section or departmental responsibilities, or have worked in the industry for a year, or have undertaken 48 weeks of recorded work experience (for those intending to study full time). They must also have gained the Professional Certificate or have appropriate experience or hold a BTEC National Diploma or a SCOTVEC National Certificate in Hotel, Catering and Institutional Operations; BTEC Continuing Education Certificate in Hospitality Management or HCIMA qualifications.

HCIMA's own examinations are divided into part A courses covering part-time or block-release based subjects studied over a period of two years, and part B courses available on a one-year full-time basis for those with at least one year's industrial experience. TEC Diplomas and BTEC National Diplomas in Hotel, Catering and Institutional Operations may obtain entry to Part B. Details of courses and colleges are available from HCIMA.

Confederation of Tourism, Hotel and Catering Management

An independent non-profit making examining body, the Confederation's principal aim is to set and maintain standards of education through the provision of course syllabuses and examinations. The CTHCM offers comprehensive schemes designed to provide people with a broad-based training in all aspects of the industry, with particular emphasis on the skills required for work in hotels and similar establishments at junior management level. There are four grades of membership: student, associate, full member and fellow. Examinations are: Certificate in Tourism; Certificate in Catering; Diploma in Tourism and Hotel Management; Diploma and Advanced Diploma in Tourism, Hotel and Catering Management; Diploma and Advanced Diploma in Professional Cookery. Single subjects include Certificate in Bakery and Sugarcraft. The certificate courses are part time, approximately six months; diploma courses are full time, six months to one year; advanced diploma courses are full time for one year.

Further details from CTHCM, 204 Barnett Wood Lane, Ashtead, Surrey KT21 2DB.

European Catering Association (Great Britain)

The ECA (GB) acts as spokesman for people involved in the business of welfare catering, this being the largest sector of the catering industry. Its aims include being a source of up-to-date information on catering trends, legislation and new products, and assisting with the education and training in the business and welfare sector of the industry. Student membership is open to all students and trainees taking approved courses in catering; the Association provides industrial experience for students, sponsorship schemes and annual competitions for catering colleges.

For further details contact the General Secretary at: ECA, 1 Victoria Parade, by 331 Sandycombe Road, Richmond, Surrey TW9 3NB.

Institute of Home Economics

The Institute is the national professional body for home economists in the UK. Corporate membership is available to graduates in home economics and holders of certain recognised qualifications with appropriate work experience. Student members are welcomed. The Institute has been involved in the development of courses by City and Guilds, BTEC and at degree level. Links between craft, technician and degree courses are established to enable a career progression of continued education. Home economists are employed by business and industry in food manufacture and, in the communications industry, in food photography. A booklet *Careers in Home Economics* is available from the Institute of Home Economics, Aldwych House, 71–91 Aldwych, London WC2B 4HN.

National Examining Board for Supervisory Management

With the encouragement of the Department of Education and Science, the NEBSS was set up in 1964 to provide examinations for foremen, supervisors and management in catering. It is an independent body administered by the City and Guilds of London Institute and its name is now as shown above.

It offers an NVQ in Management at Levels 3 and 4, as well as the following awards.

Courses

Introductory
This lasts a minimum of 30 hours only and seeks to provide background knowledge on supervisory management, including information on cost awareness, training, managing resources, and computers.

Certificate in Supervisory Management
This is for students and management, and requires 240 hours of study, including at least two days' full time. It includes a project, industrial relations, and economic and financial aspects of catering supervision.

Diploma in Supervisory Management
This is open to those who have successfully passed the certificate course or equivalent and have at least three years' experience, two of them in a supervisory capacity. It requires a minimum of 180 hours' study. For further information contact: NEBSM, 76 Portland Place, London W1N 4AA.

Royal Institute of Public Health and Hygiene

The Royal Institute offers courses for both the Primary Certificate in Hygiene for Food Handlers, and the Certificate in Food Hygiene and the Handling of Food, and more advanced diplomas. Successful diploma course candidates may qualify as members of the Institute (MRIPHH). For further information contact: the Secretary, RIPHH, 28 Portland Place, London W1N 4DE.

Royal Society of Health

The society awards a Diploma in Nutrition in relation to catering management and a Certificate in Nutrition in relation to catering and cooking, both designed for food supervisors, managers and others engaged in large-scale catering and cooking; also a Certificate in Essential Food Hygiene, a Diploma in Food Hygiene Management and a Certificate in the Hygiene of

Food Retailing and Catering designed for those engaged in the catering and food distributive and manufacturing trades. Further details of qualifications and membership from: The Royal Society of Health, RSH House, 38A St George's Drive, London SW1V 4BH.

Institute of Food Science and Technology

Certain college courses, such as HNC/HND Science (Technology of Food) give direct entry to Licentiate membership of the Institute. Courses, colleges and information about sponsorship are listed in the booklet *Where to study for a Career in Food Science and Technology;* information about types of work is given in *Careers in Food Science and Technology,* from the Institute: write to IFST, 5 Cambridge Court, 210 Shepherd's Bush Road, London W6 7NL (please enclose C5 sae).

The Wine and Spirit Education Trust Ltd

An independent charity set up to educate all those engaged in the wine and spirit trade, the Trust organises courses, sets examinations and standards, and liaises closely with the main catering bodies. It has developed with the HCTC a pack of material to train wine waiters.

Courses

Certificate course
For those with little or no knowledge of the wine trade, this is a 14-hour course divided into seven two-hour sessions and covering the history of wine; light wines of France, Italy, Germany and non-EC countries; sparkling wines, fortified wines, beers, ciders and perries, spirits and liqueurs.

Higher certificate course
This is a 30-hour course, available either full time (one week) or part time. It covers the legal aspects of wine, French wines in detail, as well as German, Italian and non-EC wines, port and madeira, cognac, whisky and liqueurs. There is an exam at the end which involves tasting the wines under discussion.

Diploma course
For those who have passed the higher certificate course, there is

a two-year diploma course. Part A (first year) and B (second year) each requiring a minimum of 200 hours' study. Successful candidates are exempt from part A of the alcoholic beverages examination of the HCIMA, and the diploma is required entry for the master of wine examination. Further information can be obtained from: the Wine and Spirit Education Trust Ltd, Five Kings House, 1 Queen Street Place, London EC4R 1QS, or from one of the regional associations who organise Trust courses in their areas.

Midland Regional Manager, Wine and Spirit Education Trust
Mrs June Grant, The Cottage, Post Office Lane, Plungar, Notts NG13 0JL

North West Wine and Spirit Association
Catherine Parkes, 20 Curzon Close, Curzon Park, Chester CH4 8AT

Eastern Counties Wine and Spirit Trade Association
F R Leatherdale, 'Beech House', Norwich Road, Long Stratton, Norfolk NR15 2PG

East Midlands Wine and Spirit Merchants' Association
c/o Andrew Hill, George Hill Ltd, 59 Wards End, Loughborough, Leics LE11 3HB

Midlands Wine and Spirit Association
Mrs Perry, Bablake Wines, Bablake House, Kingfield Road, Coventry CV1 4LD

West of England Wine and Spirit Association
G Bull, 13 Henleaze Park Drive, Bristol BS9 4LH

Education Convenor of Scotland
Graham Robertson, T M Robertson and Son Ltd, Lower Gilmore Place, Edinburgh EH3 93A

The Wine and Spirit Association of Scotland
R Leitch, 147 Bath Street, Glasgow G2 4SN

Yorkshire Wine and North East Spirit Association
Crown Chambers, 14a Princes Street, Harrogate HG1 1NJ

Eire Wine Development Board
Jean Smullen, 33 Clarinda Park West, Dun Laoghaire, Co Dublin, Eire

The British Institute of Innkeeping

One of the award-making bodies for the National Council for Vocational Qualifications, the BII has three grades of membership: Student, Associate and Member, and four examinations: Certificate of Induction, Qualifying Examination, Business Management Programme and the Membership Examination. For further details contact: British Institute of Innkeeping, 51–53 High Street, Camberley, Surrey GU15 3RG.

Caterer & Hotelkeeper

The *Caterer & Hotelkeeper* magazine has an information line on 0898 373737, open from 9.30 am to 4.30 pm on weekdays. Copies of information that has appeared in the magazine can be sent, at a minimum cost of £5, or members of the public are welcome to use the library. The magazine's last issue in January (£1.35) publishes a career guide that includes a list of colleges and directory of companies with their recruitment needs; additional copies of the guide are £1. Contact: *Caterer & Hotelkeeper*, Reed Business Publishing Group, Quadrant House, The Quadrant, Sutton, Surrey SM2 5AS.

Chapter 7
Other Careers in Catering

The purpose of this chapter is to give some indication of other jobs that are available in catering. Supposing you are a better photographer than you are a cook and have an interest in the presentation of food, then a job as a catering photographer might suit you. There are some cookery schools that specialise in training people for this purpose (see Chapter 11).

Cake Designer

A typical cake designer may provide cakes for weddings, birthdays and other special occasions. Most provide the finished, iced cake; some just bake the cake to whatever shape is required and the customer or the shop will ice it. Cake designers usually work at home, either selling their cakes from home or having an arrangement with a particular shop. Sometimes a bakery will offer and take orders for cakes, but the work will be done by a freelance cake maker at home.

Cookery Editor

Publishers of cookery books and cookery magazines require staff who have the necessary editorial skills, are able to write, and are interested in cookery.

Case Study
Martha is sub-editor on a weekly cookery partwork which is a two-year project providing recipes of a very high standard – almost gourmet, but not quite.

Martha was always interested in cookery as a hobby but did not explore the idea of cookery as a career. She took a degree in anthropology and museum science at City College, New York, and spent a further year at graduate school in Texas. She came to London to work as a volunteer at the Museum of Mankind.

I met the managing director of a publishing house at a German evening class and he offered me a job in his business/education/new technology house. First I was collecting information, then I began to do some editing and took on the editing of two magazines, and also *The World Food Book* which, incidentally, is nothing to do with cookery.

I think I obtained my present job because of my enthusiasm and the fact that I own so many cookery books - nearly 100.

I am responsible for just one piece of the partwork - the article about ingredients which I commission (find an author). I put the article into our correct house style, read the proofs when they come back, and cut bits here and there to make sure the words fit the space allowed. What I like about my present job is that it is cookery; I do miss the fact that I do not have overall responsibility for anything - the editor has final responsibility and I see only a small part. Another good thing, apart from the salary and hours (4½-day week) and the friendly atmosphere, is the fact that I can suggest recipes.

I would like to stay on after the partwork is finished; I could see myself doing this kind of work for a long time and perhaps advancing to deputy editor and editor.

Cookery is still my chief hobby, and because of my job and the beautiful photographs we have, I am far more aware of presentation than I would have been otherwise. My own favourite meal would be a salad starter or vegetables *à la Grêque*, a beef casserole with wine, served with pasta, and then my special chocolate mousse gateau - baked chocolate mousse mix sandwiched with dried apricots and fresh cream.

Cookery Journalist

Most newspapers and women's magazines have their own cookery writers. Some are trained cooks who have later become journalists; others are trained journalists with a strong interest in cookery. The National Council for the Training of Journalists runs a one-year course for prospective journalists in the periodical industry. For full details write to: The NCTJ, Latton Bush Centre, Southern Way, Harlow, Essex CM18 7BL.

Catering Photographer

Today some photographers specialise in photographing food. They have a kitchen in their studio, and will sometimes provide a cook if the client wishes. Some will also provide accessories: plates, dishes, tablecloths etc. The difficult part of the job is the preparation of food for photography. Experienced catering photographers have a number of ways of making the food look appealing and stopping it from melting under powerful arc lamps. There is nothing worse than a photograph of congealed gravy or tired looking lettuce!

To be a good catering photographer, as well as photographic skills, attention to detail and split-second timing are very important.

Catering Consultant

The Yellow Pages contain names and addresses of catering consultancy firms. Of the consultants employed by them, some work freelance; others are employed by large contract caterers to give advice on the layout of new kitchens, new equipment, staff hiring and management, and many other factors involved in the industry.

Stallholder

Catering at country fairs has many drawbacks. Some people are reluctant to sit down to an expensive meal and are looking for a quick snack. One idea which proved to be a great success was the selling of pancakes for 50p each in a paper wrapper. Plates and cutlery are not required. The overheads are eggs, flour and sugar, and a few other simple ingredients. The cooking is done on a small portable gas stove. Stalls may be set up, with permission, at country fairs, university graduation days and fêtes. Other ideas for stalls include the selling of hot potatoes, pizzas, wine and sandwiches.

Running Your Own Market Stall (Kogan Page) sets out the legal requirements for selling food from a stall.

Chapter 8
Applying for a Job

Youth Training

Youth Training (YT) gives 16-year-old school-leavers two years of training, and 17-year-old leavers one year. The two-year YT has a minimum of 20 weeks' off-the-job training, usually at colleges, training centres or workshops; one-year YT has at least seven weeks. It is organised by managing agents who may be employers, training organisations, local authorities or colleges of further education, and each trainee receives a training agreement covering training programmes and conditions of service. During the first year, trainees receive £29.50 per week and during the second year, £35 per week plus a travel allowance if fares are over £3 a week.

A permanent position is not guaranteed by the employer at the end of the year, but 70 per cent of YT participants are offered one. Application should be made through a local Jobcentre or TEC, or careers officer, but for those still at school, the careers teacher can supply preliminary information.

General Information

There are two magazines which are particularly important for people who are looking for jobs in hotel and catering work. They are: *Caterer and Hotelkeeper* and *Hospitality*. Look in the *Morning Advertiser* for jobs in the licensed trade.

Employing the right strategy can make all the difference to your success in applying for jobs. Being well organised right from the start really will pay dividends. Applying for jobs, filling in application forms and going for interviews can be boring, time consuming and often very depressing, but you must not allow any of this to affect either your applications or your manner at interviews. *Force yourself* to take the time to compose a good letter of application – a sloppy, badly written one will only end up in the waste-paper basket.

Force yourself to take time over your curriculum vitae (see pages 69–71) making sure that it is neat, accurate, and has all the relevant facts included. *Force yourself* to think about the interview. If you remember that there is a technique both to holding interviews and to being interviewed, it will help. We give a checklist of points to remember for interviews, as well as a short guide on how interviews are conducted, so that you can anticipate questions. Once you have grasped the general pattern of interviews, you will find them less confusing and frightening. And remember, never turn down the chance of going for an interview. The more practice you have at being interviewed, the better.

Springboard

Springboard is a jobcentre for the hotel and catering industry in London. It offers a comprehensive advice and information service about the types of work available, various routes into employment and training, and vacancies in the London area. It also distributes details to all London Jobcentres. Springboard is at 1 Denmark Street, London WC2H 8LP; 071-497 8654; Jobcentre: 071-497 2047.

Wages

When Wages Councils are abolished, towards the end of 1993, there will be no statutory minimum wage. At present (1992–93) the legal minimum rates agreed for those aged over 21 are: for licensed non-residential £3.01 per hour for the first 39 hours and overtime rates of £4.51 after that period; for unlicensed places of refreshment, licensed residential and licensed restaurants, £2.92 and overtime rates of £4.38. An accommodation rate (not including meals or drinks) of 20p to £2.85 per day may be deducted for live-in staff.

There is no minimum rate for trainees and those under 21. Rates for these categories at present depend on the contract negotiated between the individual employee and employer – and this will be the situation for all staff when the Wages Council is no longer in operation.

Letter of Application

□ Do a rough draft of the letter first to make sure that you have covered all essential points.

- ☐ Give details of your qualifications and experience (your curriculum vitae) on a separate sheet. See p 70 for how to lay out your curriculum vitae.
- ☐ Make absolutely sure that there are no spelling mistakes or grammatical errors in your letter. If in any doubt, ask a friend to look it over for you.
- ☐ Use good quality writing paper for your letter.
- ☐ Keep your letter brief and to the point. Mention where you saw the advertisement.
- ☐ Keep a copy of your letter for reference.

Curriculum Vitae

See p 70 for how to lay out your curriculum vitae. It should give:

- ☐ full name and address
- ☐ date of birth
- ☐ schools attended
- ☐ examinations passed
- ☐ any other honours won at school
- ☐ any particular position of authority held at school, eg school captain
- ☐ training courses or colleges attended and qualifications gained
- ☐ previous jobs held or any other experience gained
- ☐ present employment, if any
- ☐ names and addresses of two referees; one of these should be a previous employer or someone who has personal knowledge of your capabilities
- ☐ personal interests/hobbies
- ☐ languages - if you have adequate written or speaking knowledge of any languages, mention it here
- ☐ if you have a current driving licence mention it here.

The Interview

You will find interviews less frightening if you remember that they all have a form and structure. The interviewer will start by putting you at ease, making small talk about the weather or the trains.

He will then try to draw you out by asking about your career to date, what you have been doing since you left school etc. He wants you to talk so that he can get an impression of what you

MARY BROWN
32 PARK AVENUE, MANCHESTER M3 5AW

Tel: 061-123 4567

DATE OF BIRTH: ....

AGE NOW: ....

SCHOOLS ATTENDED:

   (Name and town)   (From) — (To)

COLLEGES ATTENDED:

   (Name and town)   (From) — (To)

QUALIFICATIONS:

   (Name of examination)   (Subject)   (Grade)

(Include all school/college examinations which you
have passed and any other qualifications/certificates
you have which you think would be relevant or of interest
to employers)

POSITIONS HELD:

INTERESTS AND ACTIVITIES:

FURTHER EDUCATIONAL PLANS:

EXPERIENCE:

(Start with your current job and work backwards)

REFERENCES:

(1) (Name of referee)   (Address)   (Tel no)

(2)

(3)

are like, but beware of rambling on for too long. He will then probably move on to your letter or application form and go over the details. It is important not to become bored or irritated at this point. All the things he is asking may already be there on the form, but tell him again, politely. Have an answer ready when he asks how you see your career developing, or what you would like to be doing in five years' time. Be ready too for the question of why you are applying for the particular job. Even if you have been sent by an agency you must still make it sound as if *you* are keen on the job and want to apply for it. He will probably then ask if you have a clear picture of the job and what it entails. This is to see if you have really thought about it. At the end, he will probably ask if *you* have any questions, and you must try to think of something to say. If it looks as if you are going to be offered the job, this could be the point to clear up anything you are not sure about. We give below some points to watch under 'Accepting a Job'. This would be the moment to ask to see the place of work, if you have not already done so, and to clear up any queries about salary, holidays, pension rights etc.

Checklist of Points to Remember
Remember that for most jobs your appearance, manner and general level of education will be as important as your practical skills. General points to bear in mind are:

- Be on time for the interview. If you are even five minutes late it will be a black mark against you, so leave in plenty of time, allowing for traffic jams, trains being late etc.
- Make sure you are well groomed - no messy hair, dirty shoes, grubby fingernails.
- Dress neatly rather than flashily. Avoid heavy perfumes, low necklines or very high heels.
- Smile pleasantly and look directly at the interviewer.
- Don't smoke unless invited to do so.
- Speak clearly without mumbling. Don't say 'sort of' or 'don't know' every other word.
- Don't giggle or make joking remarks.
- Be honest about your abilities.
- Never make snide or disparaging remarks about a previous employer.
- Don't allow yourself to get angry or irritated at anything the interviewer says. The interviewer may be finding out how

well you stand up to pressure, so try to keep cool and unfussed no matter how the conversation goes.

☐ Don't pick a fight with the interviewer or allow yourself to get into an argument with him, even if you know he is in the wrong.

☐ Try to avoid giving 'yes' and 'no' answers, but on the other hand don't ramble.

☐ Remember all the time that you have to sell yourself to the employer. Talk about your good points and what you can do, rather than what you can't do.

☐ Above all, try to appear interested in the job and the firm. The employer will always prefer someone who seems lively and enthusiastic.

Telephone Interviews
There is an increasing trend towards telephone interviewing. The employer does the preliminary interview over the telephone and then may ask you to come along for a more formal interview. Or, having gone for a preliminary interview, you may be rung up by the personnel officer for a background chat. In either event, it is most important that you should be well prepared.

Always remember:

☐ Write out all the relevant details about yourself on a piece of paper in case you become flustered – school, exams passed, qualifications for the job, training courses completed etc.

☐ Try to speak in a firm, clear voice. Don't mumble and 'um' and 'er' and say 'sort of' or 'you know' every other word. Your voice is the only thing the employer has to go on, so you must try to sound pleasant, self-assured and capable. Take a deep breath and try not to gabble through nerves.

☐ Come straight to the point. 'I'm ringing about the advertisement in today's paper. It sounds very interesting. Could you tell me more about it please?'

☐ If you are ringing from a call-box, make sure you have a phone card or an ample supply of coins.

Checklist of Questions to be Prepared for
The interviewer is sure to ask some, if not all, of these questions – make sure you have your answers prepared.

☐ What made you decide to go in for a catering career?
☐ What made you apply for this job?
☐ What makes you think you will be good at this job?

- What particularly attracts you about this job?
- How would you like your career to develop/What would you like to be doing in about five years' time?
- What do you like doing in your spare time?
- Tell me about your family.
- (if you already have a job) Why do you want to leave your present job?

Accepting a Job

Before you get your contract of employment, before you even write a letter of acceptance, you should make sure you know your position. No one should accept a job without understanding what it entails, what the hours and rate of pay are and what the holiday entitlement is. If you have any doubts or queries now is the time to clear them up. It is no use saying later that you didn't realise what the job involved, or that you thought you were entitled to four weeks' holiday when it turns out to be two.

Contract of Employment

A contract of employment exists as soon as someone offers you a full-time job (even verbally) at a certain rate of pay and you accept. Within 13 weeks of your starting work the employer is required by law to give you written details of your contract. These cover:

- names of the employer and employee
- job title
- date the employment began
- pay
- how you are paid (weekly, monthly etc)
- hours of work
- holiday entitlement and pay
- length of notice
- disciplinary and grievance procedures (if employer has 20 or more employees)
- pension rights
- rules about sick leave, injury and sick pay.

If you are not given a copy of your contract within 13 weeks of joining a firm, you should ask for it. The contract of employment is a legal document, so make sure that you keep it in a safe place.

Part 2

Chapter 9

Degree and Postgraduate Courses

Because of the demand for qualified management in hotels and catering firms, degree courses are very popular. Catering graduates are still sought by many organisations. For candidates with A levels, staying on to take a degree is an excellent way to start a career in catering.

Birmingham College of Food, Tourism and Creative Studies
Faculty of Hospitality Management, Summer Row, Birmingham B3 1JB; NVQ Programmes 021-604 1000 ext 239; BTEC, degree and postgraduate; 021-604 1000 ext 263
Offers a BA(Hons) in Hotel Business Management in conjunction with de Montfort University, and a further postgraduate Diploma in Hospitality Management in conjunction with the University of Birmingham. The faculty also offers full-time BTEC National and Higher National Diplomas, a part-time BTEC HNC and several NVQs at different levels.

Blackpool and The Fylde College
Department of Hotel and Food Studies, Park Road, Blackpool FY1 4JN; 0253 52352
A BA(Hons) in Hospitality Management in conjunction with the University of Central Lancashire is available, as well as a BA in Hotel, Catering and Institutional Management with Lancaster University. Also several other qualifications at different levels are on offer including a full-time BTEC First Diploma, National Diploma and HND, a BTEC part-time National Certificate and a variety of NVQs.

Bournemouth University
Department of Service Industries, Talbot Campus, Fern Barrow, Bournemouth BH1 3JJ; 0202 524111
Offers three graduate degree courses: BSc(Hons) in Food and Catering Management, BA(Hons) in Hospitality Management and BA(Hons) in Tourism Studies. As well as these there are other courses available including BTEC HND and two postgraduate degrees, an MBA in

International Hospitality/Tourism Management and an MA in European Tourism Management/Tourism Management.

University of Brighton
Department of Service Sector Management, 49 Darley Road, Eastbourne BN20 7UR; 0273 643614
The University provides a BA(Hons) in International Hospitality/Tourism Management and a BA(Hons) in Food Retailing Management/Management and Food Studies/Management and Travel Industry Studies.

Cardiff Institute of Higher Education
Faculty of Tourism, Hospitality and Food, Colchester Road, Cardiff CF3 7XR; 0222 551111
Provides only one degree course: a BA(Hons) in Hotel Management/Tourism/Recreation and Leisure. However, it does offer a wide range of BTEC awards including full-time First, National and Higher National Diplomas and part-time First National and Higher National Certificates. NVQs are also available.

University of Central England in Birmingham
Department of Management, Perry Barr, Birmingham B42 2SU; 021-235 2157/331 5200
BA(Hons) in Hospitality Management.

University of Central Lancashire
Department of Organisation Studies, Preston PR1 2HE; 0772 893770
Offers one BA(Hons) degree in Hospitality Management, and another in Hospitality Operations and Management, which is in conjunction with Blackpool and the Fylde College. There is also available a postgraduate degree in Tourism, Leisure and Service Management.

Cheltenham and Gloucester College of Higher Education
Department of Leisure Management, Francis Close Hall Campus, Swindon Road, Cheltenham GL50 4AZ; 0242 532824
The college offers two degrees: a BA(Hons) in Hotel/Tourism/Leisure Management and a BSc(Hons) in Catering Management. There is also available an MA in Leisure and Tourism and a full-time BTEC HND.

Clarendon College
Department of Catering and Hospitality Management, Pelham Avenue, Nottingham NG5 1AL; 0602 691418
The College offers a BA(Hons) in International Hospitality Management and many other qualifications at different levels. These include part time HCIMA Professional Certificates and Diplomas, BTEC full-time Diplomas and part-time Certificates, and several NVQ awards.

The Colchester Institute
School of Hotel and Catering Studies, Sheepen Road, Colchester, Essex CO3 3LL; 0255 220444 (degree and HND); 0206 761660 (other courses)
BA Business Studies (Catering Management). The Institute also offers some full-time BTEC awards including a First Diploma, National Certificate/Diploma and HND. A selection of NVQs is also available.

Derby Tertiary College
Catering Section, London Road, Wilmerton, Derby DE24 8UG; 0332 757570
BSc(Hons) in Hospitality Management. The college also offers a BTEC National Diploma which can be taken full or part time. NVQs are also available.

Duncan of Jordanstone College with the University of Dundee
School of Food and Accommodation Management, Perth Road, Dundee DD1 4HT; 0382 23261
MA(Hons) in Hotel and Catering Management, also HNC/D, full time (SCOTVEC).

Herefordshire College of Technology
Department of Hospitality, Tourism and Leisure, Folly Lane, Hereford HR1 1LS; 0432 352235
Subject to approval a degree in Leisure Management will be on offer. In addition there is a postgraduate degree in Tourism and International Commerce, validated by the University of Lille, and several other different level courses including an HCIMA Professional Diploma and a Certificate, full-time BTEC First Diploma, National Diploma and an HND subject to approval. Several NVQs are also on offer.

Highbury College
Faculty of Business, Management and Hospitality Studies, Dovercourt Road, Cosham, Portsmouth PO6 2SA; 0705 383131
Offers a BA(Hons) in Hotel and Catering Management and a variety of different level courses including a postgraduate degree in Hospitality Management, a full-time BTEC HND, a part-time BTEC HNC, a GNVQ and several NVQs.

University of Huddersfield
Department of Food, Nutrition and Hospitality Management, Queensgate, Huddersfield HD1 3DH; 0484 422288
A choice of graduate degrees is available, namely a BA(Hons) in Hotel and Catering Business, BA(Hons) in International Hospitality Management/Hotel and Catering Management with Leisure and Tourism, and a BSc(Hons) in Catering and Applied Nutrition/Food and Nutrition.

The University also offers a further MBA in Hospitality Management and a full-time BTEC HND.

University of Humberside
Nun's Corner, Grimsby, Humberside DN34 5BQ; 0482 440550
HND Food Science/Food Technology. Three-year sandwich course for those with at least one A level or a National Diploma. Other courses include a BSc(Hons) in European Food Studies, a BSc(Hons) in Food Industry Management, a BSc(Hons) Food Science (Food Quality and Control); a BSc(Hons) in Food Technology; a BSc(Hons) in Nutrition Studies, a Foundation Year (extended degrees in Food Studies and Nutrition Studies).

Leeds Metropolitan University
Leisure and Consumer Studies Programme Area, City Campus, Calverley Street, Leeds LS1 3HE; 0532 832600
Offers a BSc in Hospitality Management and Related Sectors, a BA in Hospitality Business/Tourism/Leisure Management, and a BSc in Catering Technology Management (from 1994). Also available is a further MSc in Hospitality Management and a full- or part-time BTEC HND.

Leith's Good Food
86 Bondway, London SW8 1SF; 071-735 6296 (Jill Spencer, Personnel and Training Manager)
Catering company including contract catering. College sponsorship for craft students, as well as post-college training programme for C&G qualifications giving experience in different divisions including Leith's Restaurant. One-year management training scheme for HND/degree students.

The Manchester Metropolitan University
Department of Hotel, Catering and Tourism Management, Hollings Faculty, Old Hall Lane, Manchester M14 6HR; 061-247 2722
The Hollings Faculty of Manchester Metropolitan University contains one of the largest hotel and catering departments in the country; there are four courses.

1. BSc in Hotel and Catering Services, four-year sandwich course. In the first two years, subjects studied are operational management (food and accommodation), administration (information technology, accounts and management), business environment (economics, law and behavioural studies).
2. Postgraduate Diploma/MSc in Hotel and Catering Studies. One year. During the year a period of four weeks is spent in industry and the subjects studied include food and beverage management, accommo-

dation management and hygiene, plus four weeks' industrial placement. It is necessary to write a 5,000-word dissertation.
3. BTEC HND in Hotel Catering and Institution Management, three-year sandwich course with one term in each of the first and second years spent in industry. Each course year lasts 36 weeks and is based on modules, which are accommodation operations, food and beverage production and service, premises and plant, front office, applied science, maths, law, economics, purchasing, finance, marketing management, manpower studies, information technology and projects.
4. HCIMA Professional Examination Part B. Day-release course is available. Those passing the four-year BSc course are exempt from both HCIMA A and B exams and thus eligible for professional membership after two years' post-qualification experience.

Middlesex University
School of Management, The Burroughs, Hendon, London NW4 4BT; 081-362 5000
BA(Hons) in Hotel and Restaurant Management.

Napier University
Hospitality and Tourism Management, Merchiston Site, 10 Colinton Road, Edinburgh EH10 5DT; 031-455 2571/444 2266
Offers a BA/BA(Hons) in Hospitality (Hotel and Catering Management). Further to this it also provides a PgD/MSc in Hospitality (Hotel and Catering Management) and a PgD/MSc in Hospitality (Technology Management). A full-time SCOTVEC HND is also available.

University of North London
School of Leisure, Tourism, Hotel and Catering Management, Holloway Road, London N7 8DB; 071-607 2789
Offers a BA(Hons) in Hotel and Catering/International Hotel and Catering Management and a full-time BTEC HND.

Norwich City College of Further and Higher Education
Norwich Hotel School, Ipswich Road, Norwich NR2 2LJ; 0603 660011 ext 277 (Carole Williams, Education Liaison Officer)
The Hotel School offers a BA(Hons) in Hospitality Management, four years sandwich; BTEC HND Hotel, Catering and Institutional Management, two or three years sandwich. HCIMA Professional Qualification (flexible learning) and full range of craft and technician programmes.

Nottingham Trent University
Nottingham Business School – Postal Address: Burton Street, Nottingham NG1 4BU; Visiting Department: Chaucer Building, City Centre Site; 0602 486414/418418
A BA(Hons) in Hotel and Catering/International Hospitality Manage-

ment is available, as well as an MA in Tourism/Business Administration (Hospitality Enterprise). Also on offer are a full-time BTEC HND and part-time HNC.

Oxford Brookes University
School of Hotel and Catering Management, Gypsy Lane, Headington, Oxford OX3 0BP; 0865 819800
Offers a BSc(Hons) in Hotel and Catering Management and a combined BSc/BA(Hons) in Catering Management, with another field to be chosen from a wide range, including Tourism, Retail Management, Nutrition etc. There is opportunity to take a further MSc and/or postgraduate degree on block release. A full-time HCIMA Professional Diploma is also available.

Plymouth College of Further Education
Department of Hotel, Catering and Tourism Studies, Kings Road, Davenport, Plymouth PL1 5QG; 0752 385888
Plymouth College offers a BSc in Hospitality Management in conjunction with the University of Plymouth and South Devon College. It also offers full-time BTEC First, National and Higher National Diplomas, as well as a variety of NVQs and a part-time HCIMA Professional Certificate.

University of Plymouth
Seale-Hayne Faculty of Agriculture, Food and Land Use, Department of Food Studies, Newton Abbot, Devon TQ12 6NQ; 0626 325643/325606
BSc(Hons) in Hospitality Management.

Portsmouth Business School, University of Portsmouth
Locksway Road, Milton, Southsea, Portsmouth PO4 8JF; 0705 827681
BA(Hons) in Hotel and Catering Management and a postgraduate degree in Hotel and Catering Management are available.

Queen Margaret College
Department of Hospitality Studies, Clerwood Terrace, Edinburgh EH12 8TS; 031-317 3000/3247
A BA in Hospitality Enterprise with Tourism is available, together with a PgD in Hospitality Management, an HCIMA Professional Diploma (distance learning subject to approval) and a full-time SCOTVEC HND.

The Queen's College
School of Hospitality Management, 1 Park Drive, Glasgow G3 6LP; 041-337 4000
Offers a BA/BA(Hons) in Hospitality Management, together with a further PgD in Hospitality Management and a full-time SCOTVEC HND.

Reid Kerr College
Department of Catering Studies, Renfrew Road, Paisley PA3 4DR;
041-889 4225
Offers a BSc/HND in Quality Management and Technology for Hospitality in association with Paisley University. Also available is a range of full- or part-time SCOTVEC awards including National Certificates, HNCs and an HND (subject to approval). Several SVQs are also available at differing levels.

The Robert Gordon University
School of Food and Consumer Studies, Queen's Road, Aberdeen AB9 2PG; 0224 633611
A full-time BA/BA(Hons) in Hospitality Management is available, and also a full-time SCOTVEC HND.

University College Salford
Department of Food and Consumer Studies, Frederick Road, Salford M6 6PU; 061-736 6541
Offers a BA(Hons) in Hospitality Management and several other qualifications at differing levels. These include a full-time HCIMA Professional Certiicate, full- or part-time BTEC National Certificate, a full-time BTEC National Diploma, a full-time BTEC HND and several NVQs.

Sheffield Hallam University
School of Leisure and Food Management, Pond Street, Sheffield S1 1WB; 0742 533325 (Sheila Robson)
Full range of courses including HND Home Economics; HND Hotel, Catering and Institutional Management; BSc(Hons) Food Marketing Management (four years sandwich); BSc(Hons) Hotel and Catering Management (four years sandwich); BA(Hons) Home Economics (four years sandwich); MA/PgDip/PgCert Food Management and Hospitality Management.

South Bank University
National Centre for Hotel Management, 103 Borough Road, London SE1 0AA; 071-928 8989
BA(Hons) in Hotel Management.

South Devon College
Department of Hotel and Catering, Newton Road, Torquay TQ2 5BY; 0803 217511
Offers a BSc in Hospitality Management in conjunction with the University of Plymouth. As well as this, it also offers a wide range of full- or part-time BTEC and HCIMA Higher and Lower Diplomas and Certificates (flexible learning subject to approval). NVQs are also available.

Stafford College

Directorate of Hotel, Catering, Tourism and Leisure, Earl Street, Stafford ST16 2QR; 0785 223800

A BA(Hons) in Hotel, Tourism and Licensed Retail Management, in association with the University of Wolverhampton, is available. The College also offers a range of full-time BTEC Diplomas and part-time Certificates including a full- or part-time HND. Several NVQs are also on offer.

University of Strathclyde

Scottish Hotel School, Curran Building, 94 Cathedral Street, Glasgow G4 0LG; 041-552 4400 ext 3954

Offers a BA/BA(Hons) in Hotel and Catering Management, together with a PgD/MSc in Hotel Administration and a PgD/MSc/PhD in Tourism.

University of Surrey

Guildford, Surrey GU2 5XH; 0483 571281

BSc in Hotel and Catering Management; four years, one year spent in industry. Applicants should have a minimum of three O levels and two A levels, and their subjects offered should include another European language, mathematics, English and a science subject. Most candidates nowadays, however, can offer three A levels. The course content is as follows: Stages 1 and 2 – four main areas of study: management, quantitative studies, food and beverage management and business studies. Stage 3 (BSc Hons only) – hotel and catering management, finance management, marketing, food and nutrition, and tourism plus a project.

BSc in Hotel Management, three years. A course for candidates from overseas.

Postgraduate Courses: Diploma MSc in Tourism Studies, one year; MSc in International Hotel Management.

Thames Valley University

School of Hospitality Studies, St Mary's Road, London W5 5RF; 081-579 5000

The University offers a BA(Hons) in Hospitality Management with a further postgraduate degree in the same subject. There is also available a range of courses at differing levels including full- and part-time BTEC National Diplomas, HNCs and HNDs, a part-time HCIMA Professional Certificate, and a variety of NVQs.

University of Ulster

Department of Hotel and Catering Management, Shore Road, Newtownabbey, Co Antrim BT38 0QB; 0232 365131

Two degrees are available: a BA(Hons) in Hospitality Management and a BA(Hons) in Hotel and Tourism Management (at Magee campus).

There is also an MSc/PgD in Hotel and Catering Management and a full-time BTEC HND.

University of Wales, College of Cardiff
School of Home Economics and Institutional Management, 65–67 Park Place, Cardiff CF1 3AS; 0222 874846
Offers a BSc in Hotel and Institutional Management, as well as a PgD/MSc in Tourism.

University of Wolverhampton
Wolverhampton Business School, Compton Road West, Compton Park, Wolverhampton WV3 9DX; 0902 323629/321000
Offers a BA(Hons) in Hotel, Tourism and Licensed Retail Management in conjunction with Stafford College. The School also provides a full-time BTEC HND and a few high-level NVQs (subject to approval).

Teacher Training for Catering

Full-time one-year courses are available for those intending to train as catering teachers at the following places. They should have recognised qualifications and work experience and/or a degree.

School of Education and Health Studies
Bolton Institute of Higher Education
Chadwick Street
Bolton BL2 1JW

University of Greenwich
Head of Food Studies Department
Downshire House
Roehampton
London SW15 4HR

University of Huddersfield
Holly Bank Road
Lindley, Huddersfield
West Yorkshire HD3 3BP

One-day block-release and evening class courses over a period of two years are available for in-service teachers in further and adult education who have not yet qualified as teachers. Courses lead to the City and Guilds Further and Adult Education Teachers Certificate and take place at around 200 approved centres throughout the country. A list of the centres is available from the City and Guilds of London Institute, 46 Britannia Street,

London WC1X 9RG. Further information is also available from the HCIMA.

Chapter 10

Career Opportunities in In-house Catering

Some of the main catering groups with in-house training schemes for staff are listed below. They all offer different opportunities and it is best to write to the addresses given to find out the most up-to-date information.

ARA Services plc
(Rosemary Walsh, 081-844 1313; Maureen Royce, 061-624 8031)
ARA House, Honey End Lane, Tilehurst, Reading, Berkshire RG3 7QL; 0734 596761

Arundel House Hotel
(Personnel and Training Manager)
Chesterton Road, Cambridge CB4 3AN; 0223 67701

Bass Leisure Ltd
(Gill Baldwin, Personnel Manager)
New Castle House, Castle Boulevard, Nottingham NG7 1FT; 0602 484333

Beefeater
(Jackie Chapman)
PO Box 31, The Halfway House, Luton Road, Dunstable, Bedfordshire LU5 4LL; 0582 660970
On-job management training scheme

B E Services Ltd
(Brian T Watts)
Bank of England, Threadneedle Street, London EC2R 8AH; 071-601 4271

Best Western Hotels
(Director of Membership Services)
Vine House, 143 London Road, Kingston upon Thames, Surrey KT2 6NA; 081-541 0050
Applications circulated to all member hotels

Boodles
(Richard Edmonds, Secretary/Manager)
St James's Street, London SW1A 1HJ; 071-930 7166
One trainee manager taken each year with minimum five GCSEs for four to five year scheme. One apprentice chef taken on for three- or four-year scheme; both live-in

Bourne Leisure Group Ltd
(Steven Mullings)
51-55 Bridge Street, Hemel Hempstead, Hertfordshire HP1 1LX; 0442 69257
Graduates in Hotel and Catering or Leisure Management. Limited number for management training scheme; training includes front of house, food and beverage, sales

Britannia Hotels
(Michael G. Marten, Group Personnel and Training Services Manager)
London Road, Manchester M1 2PH; 061-228 1271

Burger King UK
(Marina Young, Personnel Officer)
20 Kew Road, Richmond, Surrey TW9 2NA; 081-332 2200

Carnival Cruise Lines
(Bandy Coldham or Carol Benjamin)
418-422 Strand, London WC2R 0PT; 071-240 8471

Catering & Allied
(Sarah E Banner, Quality Assurance Director)
Central House, Balfour Road, Hounslow, Middlesex TW3 1HA; 081-569 4343
Opportunities for management trainees; applicants should have BTEC ND and HND. Trainee cooks with C&G 706/1 and 2.

The Catering Guild
(Nick Jones, Operations Director)
The Upper Mill, Kingston Road, Ewell, Surrey KT17 2AF; 081-394 1722

Caterleisure Ltd
(Mr P Clark)
197-199 Main Street, Wilsden, Bradford BD15 0HR; 0535 273292

CCG Catering
(Eric McNally, Personnel Director)
Steuart Road, Bridge of Allan, Stirling FK9 4JG; 0786 834060

The Chester Grosvenor
(Rosa di Mascio)
Eastgate Street, Chester CH1 1LT; 0244 324024

Compass Services (UK) Ltd
    North: Sue Kemmery, 0532 521017

Central: Jeff Rollason, 061-872 2112
West: Christ Ashcroft, 0272 264317
East: David Atkins, 0582 600222
London: Cathy Smith, 081-741 1541
Commercial Services Division: Raj Pragasam, 0252 623211
Queen's Wharf, Queen Caroline Street, London W6 9RL; 081-741 1541

Concord Hotels
(A A Thibault)
7 Green Road, Terriers, High Wycombe, Buckinghamshire HP13 5BD;
0494 523906
Personnel and training consortium

Copthorne Hotels Ltd
Victoria House, Horley, Surrey RH6 7AF; 0293 772288
Management training scheme and development policy

Croft Hotels
(Linda Wilkinson)
Ryedale Building, Piccadilly, York YO1 1PN; 0904 643399
*Three to four places on management training scheme, covers reception,
accounting, kitchen, food and beverage, sales and housekeeping*

Deep Pan Pizza
(Jenny Hagras, Personnel)
531 High Road, Wembley, Middlesex HA0 2DJ; 081-900 0955
*Trainee managers and assistant managers nationwide with catering
qualifications or background. Kitchen and waiting staff aged 18–35.
Experience an advantage but not essential; full training is provided*

De Vere Hotels
(Alan Makinson, Group Personnel Manager)
Chester Road, Daresbury, Warrington, Cheshire WA4 4BN; 0925 265050
*Recruits BTEC HND and degree graduates (or equivalent SCOTVEC)
each year for management training programmes*

Dukes Hotel
(Linda Sinclair, Personnel Manager)
35 St James's Place, London SW1A 1NY; 071-491 4840

Edwardian Hotels
(Arnie Ashmore)
140 Bath Road, Hayes, Middlesex UB3 5AW; 071-636 5601
Experience for craft positions not essential; full training given

Everards Brewery Ltd
(Ian Gibson)
Castle Acres, Narborough, Leicester LE9 5BY; 0533 630900

Fairfield Catering Company
(Mrs Jacqui Godfrey-Smith, Training Manager)

Twickenham House, 20 East Saint Helen Street, Abingdon, Oxfordshire
OX14 5EA; 0235 559955
Training programmes

First Leisure Corporation plc
(Sarah Whitehead, Group Training Manager)
7 Soho Street, London W1V 5FA; 071-437 9727

A Fistful of Tacos
(Barry Prior)
31 Albert Road, Southsea, Portsmouth, Hampshire PO5 2SE;
0705 293474

Forte Welcome Break
(Mrs Kathie Kinton)
2 Vantage Court, Tickford Street, Newport Pagnell, Buckinghamshire
MK16 9EZ; 0908 617766

Friendly Hotels plc
(Brian Worthington, Group Personnel/Training Director)
Premier House, 10 Greycoat Place, London SW1P 1SB; 071-222 8866
*Management training programmes of 9 to 15 months; 25 places for
students with BTEC HNC/D, CHIMA, SCOTVEC HNC/D or degrees*

Gardner Merchant Ltd
(Gary Palmer)
Grant House, 114 Broadway, Salford, Manchester M5 2UW;
061-876 0705

The Goring Hotel
(Shara Ross, Personnel Manager)
15 Beeston Place, Grosvenor Gardens, London SW1W 0JW;
071-834 8211

Granada Motorway Services Ltd
(Lesley Wells)
M1 Service Area, Toddington, Bedfordshire LV5 6HR; 05255 3881

Group Chez Gerard Ltd
(Debbie Jelffs)
37 Dean Street, London W1V 5AP; 071-439 2925

Happy Eater
(Ms C Headland, Personnel Manager)
Unit 2, Cartel Business Centre, Stroudley Road, Basingstoke, Hampshire
RG24 0FW; 0256 812828
*Opportunities for seasonal part-time and full-time work. Trainee
management for full-time only*

Hidden Hotels Ltd
(Hilary Davis, Training Manager)
Nutfield Priory, Nutfield, Redhill, Surrey RH1 4EN; 0737 822072

Management and department training programmes individually tailored from 6 to 18 months

Hilton United Kingdom
(Shereen Silva)
PO Box 137, Millbuck House, Clarendon Road, Watford, Hertfordshire WD1 1DN; 0923 246464
Up to 35 HND, degree and HCIMA students for individually tailored graduate development schemes of up to two years

Holiday Inn Worldwide
(Sue Hale)
UK District Office, Bridge Street, Banbury, Oxfordshire OX16 8RQ; 0295 272278
Training at all levels for school leavers, graduates or those with previous supervisory or management experience

Hotels of the Cinque Ports
(Michael Gregory)
Mermaid House, Rye, Sussex TN31 7DS; 0797 223788

Imperial London Hotels Ltd
(Mrs Barbara Wright)
Russell Square, London WC1; 071-278 3922

Instore
(Kate Robbins-Jones or Jane Rees, Personnel)
Bickler House, Tamworth Road, Croydon, Surrey CR9 1XQ; 081-680 5261

Inter-Continental and Forum Hotels
(Jacqueline Moyse, Regional Training Manager)
c/o The London Inter-Continental Hotel, 1 Hamilton Place, London W1V 0QY; 071-409 3131
Recruits at all levels: craft, BTEC and HNC/D or degree; some training places

McDonald's Restaurants Ltd
(Regional Personnel Department)
11–59 High Road, East Finchley, London N2 8AW; 081-883 6400

Metropole Hotel
(Gary Patchett)
National Exhibition Centre, Birmingham B40 1PT; 021-780 4266
Supervisory training for BTEC ND and C&G qualifications and trainee management scheme for HND, degree or HCIMA graduates. Opportunities also exist for craft-trained chefs, waiting staff, housekeepers and telephonists

Mount Charlotte Thistle Hotels
(Dianne Myers)

2 The Calls, Leeds LS2 7JU; 0532 439111
Structured training programmes to suit students with varying quali-
fications. Training scheme is six months to two years according to
qualification levels and experience

My Kinda Town
(Simon Kossoff)
195–197 King's Road, Chelsea, London SW3; 071-376 5076
Duty managers, graduate trainees and placement students, as well as
full range of staff positions. In-house training at all levels

National Leisure Catering Ltd
(Judith Lee)
Wembley Conference Centre, Wembley, London HA9 0DW; 081-902 8833
ND/HND and degree holders

P&O Cruises Ltd
(Mr P Litts, Senior Fleet Personnel Officer)
Dukes Keep, Marsh Lane, Southampton SO9 4GU; 0703 336262

Pizza Express
(Ian Eldridge)
29 Wardour Street, London W1; 071-437 7215

Princess Cruises
(Recruitment Manager)
c/o P&O Lines Ltd, Dukes Keep, Marsh Lane, Southampton, Hampshire
SO9 4GU; 0703 332500

Quadrant
(Tricia Howarth, Personnel Manager)
Contract House, Faraday Road, Swindon SN3 5HQ
Professional catering service with 3,000 employees; opportunities at
all levels. Tailor-made training covers all aspects of craft and
management skills

Queen's Moat Houses plc
(Mr I Edwards, Operations Director)
Queens Court, 9–17 Eastern Road, Romford, Essex RM1 3NG;
0708 730522

Resort Hotels plc
(Barry Warrington, Group Training and Development Manager)
Resort House, Edward Street, Brighton, East Sussex BN2 2HW;
0273 676717
Management trainee programme for BTEC HND and degree students.
Full craft training for front office, accommodation, kitchens, bar and
restaurants

Ritz Hotel
(Jeremy Davis, Personnel Manager)

150 Piccadilly, London W1V 9DG; 071-493 8181

Roadside Services Ltd
(Jim Glover, Personnel Director)
439-445 Godstone Road, Whyteleafe, Surrey CR3 0YG; 0883 623355
Career opportunities at all levels. Management training scheme open to graduates

Roper Catering Group
(Amanda Reeve)
Rose Villa Farm, Eynewbury, St Neots, Cambridgeshire PE19 2NF; 0480 72086
Regular opportunities for unit manager and chef manager. BTEC HND or HCIMA qualifications required

Royal Crescent Hotel
(David Passey, Personnel Manager)
16 Royal Crescent, Bath, Avon BA1 2LS; 0225 319090

Russell & Brand Ltd
(Joyce White)
Marqueen House, 215-251 High Street, Beckenham, Kent BR3 1BN; 081-650 2255
Management trainees who have C&G or BTEC National and Higher National Diplomas; training programme with off-job training courses. Apprentice chefs

St Davids Park Hotel
(Philippa Butcher)
St Davids Park, Ewloe, Clwyd, CH5 3YB; 0244 520800

Sbarro
(Alison Spicer, Regional Manager)
9th Floor, Great West House, Great West Road, Brentford, Middlesex TW8 9DF; 081-860 0839
BTEC HND, HCIMA or degree qualifications. Comprehensive induction and development training

Scottish Highland Hotels
(Paul Murray-Smith, Director)
98 West George Street, Glasgow G2 1PW; 041-332 3033

Selsdon Park Hotel
(Personnel Department)
Sanderstead, South Croydon, Surrey CR2 8YA; 081-657 8811

Shearings
(Mrs Jane Burke)
Miry Lane, Wigan WN3 4AG; 0942 44246

Shire Inns Ltd
(Anthony Spencer, Company Personnel Manager)

Colne Road, Reedley, Burnley, Lancashire BB10 2NG; 0282 414141
*Comprehensive training programme of small number of degree, HND
or equivalent graduates, interviewed Jan/Feb for Sept entry. Two-year
departmental programme for those with BTEC National Diploma or
equivalent*

Sports & Leisure Foods
(Clive Evans or Anne Sugden)
George Street House, Macclesfield, Cheshire SK11 6HS; 0625 610025
*Approved craft training company with own training programme.
Recruits unit managers and trainee managers*

Stafford Hotel
(Jeremy Davis, Personnel Manager)
16–18 St James's Place London SW1A 1NJ; 071-493 0111

Stakis Hotels
(Ian Cockburn)
3 Atlantic Quay, York Street, Glasgow G2 8JH; 041-204 4321
*Management training programme for students with degree or HND in
hotel/catering management*

Sutcliffe Catering Group
(Mr P W Davis)
Portland House, Aldermaston Court, Church Road, Aldermaston,
Reading, Berkshire RG7 4XS; 0734 810144

Swallow Hotels Ltd
(Rob Gilvary, Management Development Manager)
PO Box 8, Swallow House, Seaburn Terrace, Seaburn, Sunderland, Tyne
& Wear SR6 8BB; 091-529 4545

Torquay Leisure Hotels
(Mrs Trudy Bovey)
Belgrave Road, Torquay, Devon TO2 5HL; 0803 291222

Travellers Fare Ltd
(P H Duff, Personnel Manager)
50 Paul Street, London EC2A 4AE; 071-729 2200
Recruits trainee managers; individual training programmes

Vienna Group, London
(Paul Burley)
16 Leinster Square, London W2 4PR; 071-286 5294

Whitbread Inns
(Emma Coote, Training and Recruitment)
Park Square Chambers, 14 Park Street, Luton, Bedfordshire LU1 3EP

Whitbread plc
   Managed pubs: Emma Coote – see above

Thresher: Ms Jill Schoral, Thresher Wine Merchants, Ellis Ashton Street, Huyton Industrial Estate, Huyton, Liverpool L36 9UD

Restaurants and leisure: Mike Clark, Whitbread Restaurants and Leisure Division, Whitbread House, Park Street West, Luton, Bedfordshire LU1 3BG

The Brewery, Chiswell Street, London EC1Y 4SD (headquarters)

Opportunities occur regularly at all levels and are advertised in the press

Chapter 11
Private Cookery Schools

This chapter lists the majority of private cookery schools in the UK offering short courses. Some also offer three-term courses leading to their own diplomas, and 12-week certificate courses. Fees quoted are from 1993 unless otherwise stated; they should be reconfirmed on application.

The Bath School of Cookery
Bassett House, Claverton, Bath, Avon BA2 7BL; 0225 722498

Master Course, one month
Intensive course in basic techniques progressing towards more involved and complicated skills with over 100 recipes from all over the world, but mainly everyday French. Costs £990, non-resident (1993).

Also four-day courses: Introduction Course (£270); Creative Cooking Course I (£270); Creative Cooking Course II (£280); Vegetarian and Wholefood Course (£270). Costs are for non-residential courses, 1993.

The Cordon Bleu Cookery School (London) Ltd
114 Marylebone Lane, London W1M 6HH; 071-935 3503
Founded in 1933 by Rosemary Hume, the Cordon Bleu Cookery School has become internationally famous. Fees for its courses are high, but many leading personalities in the world of cooking, teachers, journalists, writers and restaurateurs are graduates of the Cordon Bleu School.

The Classic Cycle of daytime and evening training courses has three cuisine and two pâtisserie courses. It is offered throughout the year and can be completed in three terms (nine months). Students are awarded Le Diplôme de Cuisine on successful completion of the three cuisine courses. Le Diplôme de Pâtisserie is awarded on successful completion of the two pâtisserie courses. Le Grand Diplôme is awarded on successful completion of all five courses in the Classic Cycle, recognised by the best kitchens in France and throughout the world.

Cours de Cuisine de Base (Introduction to Classic Cuisine); one term of 11 weeks full time or two or three 11-week terms part time as twice-weekly evening classes; £2,395
Foundation for those who wish to gain a recognised qualification in a short space of time; designed for the future professional as well as the keen amateur. The certificate for Cuisine de Base is awarded on successful completion of the course.

Cours de Cuisine Intermédiaire (Intermediate Classic Course); one term of 11 weeks; £2,595
Students have already taken Cuisine de Base; the classical repertoire is extended. The certificate of Cuisine Intermédiaire is awarded on successful completion of the course.

Cours de Cuisine Supérieure (Superior Classic Cuisine); one term of 11 weeks; £2,800
For students to master the art of 'Haute Cuisine'; the recipes are concerned with complex techniques and the standard of dishes prepared is equal to those of Michelin star restaurants. The certificate of Cuisine Supérieure is awarded on successful completion of the course.

Cours de Pâtisserie de Base (Introduction to Pâtisserie); one term of 11 weeks full time or two or three 11-week terms as twice-weekly evening classes; £1,795
The course provides a grounding in the art of pâtisserie and can be simultaneously combined with the Cours de Cuisine de Base, or taken independently. Useful to the future professional working in a hotel, restaurant or tea-room. The certificate of Pâtisserie de Base is awarded on successful completion of the course.

Cours de Pâtisserie Avancée (Advanced Pâtisserie); one term of 11 weeks; £1,995
Progresses from the basic skills of the Cours de Pâtisserie de Base and can be combined simultaneously with the Cours de Cuisine Intermédiaire, or taken independently. The certificate for Pâtisserie Avancée is awarded on successfully completing the course,

and those who want further training can go on to the Cours de Pâtisserie Supérieure, offered only in Paris.

Specialised daytime and evening short courses and lectures include courses in Primary Food Hygiene (£80), sous-vide (cooking foods in a vacuum-seal – useful for those responsible for production kitchen facilities as well as food manufacturers) and wines (from £235).

Eastbourne College of Food and Fashion
1 Silverdale Road, Eastbourne BN20 7AA; 0323 730851

Intensive Cordon Bleu Certificate Course; one term, from £1,290 (resident students) and £2,450 (day students)
Course takes a student from basics to Cordon Bleu standard and leads to Intensive Cordon Bleu Certificate, pass, credit or distinction and includes Certificate of Wine examination. Cookery employment agencies and ski companies visit Eastbourne to interview the students.

Advanced Cordon Bleu Diploma; from £3,300 (resident students) and £2,750 (day students) per term
Students must have a minimum of Credit pass on the Eastbourne Cordon Bleu diploma or have relevant cookery experience. Includes pâtisserie and visits to top hotel and restaurant kitchens, directors' dining rooms and food preparation companies, wine appreciation seminar, and a week's work experience at a top-class hotel or restaurant.

One-year Career Cooks Course; from £3,000 (resident students) and £2,500 (day students) per term
Term one: Intensive Cordon Bleu Certificate. Term two: Advanced Cordon Bleu Diploma. Term three: Diploma in Catering and Restaurant Management. Students sit the Wine Certificate and the Food Hygiene Examination. A long block of work experience in a top-class establishment and Business Studies are arranged in term three. Students are helped to find holiday work, and are given careers guidance and help in finding work on completion of the course. Entry requirements: some previous experience, over 18.

Eastbourne Diploma Course; one year, from £2,990 (resident students) and £2,200 (day students) per term
First two foundation terms include pre-cordon bleu cookery and

catering as well as fashion, interior design, secretarial studies, flower artistry and child care. Students select from specialist options for the third term: cordon bleu, catering and restaurant management, fashion or child care. Entrance requirements: Minimum age of 16 (no upper age limit) and GCSE passes. Courses begin in September and January.

Edinburgh Cookery School
Newliston, Kirkliston, Edinburgh EH29 9EB; 031-333 1501
Comprehensive training provides skills which can lead to a career in cookery, freelance seasonal employment in shooting and fishing lodges, ski chalets, yachts and directors' dining rooms, or possibly for travelling abroad to work. Students are introduced to business studies and encouraged to consider self-employment.

One-year Diploma course comprising three Certificate courses: Highland Lodge Certificates 1, 2 and 3
The Diploma course is examined externally and independently. The Certificate courses are each offered as self-contained shorter courses and may be taken as an individual certificate or as part of the one-year diploma course. Certificate 3, the final part of the diploma course, includes new trends in cooking, healthy eating, wine appreciation, flower arranging, advanced sugarcraft and a communications course.

Four-week intensive course
Suitable for beginners or as a refresher; held in September.

Eggleston Hall
Barnard Castle, Co Durham DL12 0AG; 0833 50378
Directors: Rosemarie Gray and Victoria Straker.

Cordon Bleu Certificate course; 12 weeks. £2,700
On completing the course, students can take the Theory and Practical exam, gaining a 'Cook for Profit' Certificate. At the end of the course students go on to cook in shooting and fishing lodges, chalets, villas, directors' dining rooms and yachts in the Caribbean, and also run their own businesses.

The School also has daily practical lessons covering different aspects of cooking, from basics to more advanced skills, and also offers flower-arranging courses.

The Grange
Whatley Vineyard, Whatley, Frome, Somerset BA11 3LA; 0373 836579
Founded by Ann Norris in 1981 and set in an old coach house. Many students of Basics to Bearnaise and Beyond Bearnaise go on to work in chalets during the skiing season in Europe, America and the Antipodes, and on cruise ships in the summer. The Grange runs five different courses.

Course 1. Basics to Bearnaise, four weeks
This is a step-by-step cordon bleu course with five hours of tuition a day. A Certificate is presented at the end of the course. Cost from £1,030.

Course 2. Beyond Bearnaise, two weeks
Following Course 1, with individual menu planning. Cost £520.

Course 3. Food with Flair, four days
A 'fun' course where new-found skills can be used. This course has a French basis. Cost from £275.

Course 4. 'By special request', four days
More expensive ingredients are used and the course is shaped around four special menus.

The Chalet Course, one week
Intensive course, for those who want to work in a chalet, includes chalet-style menus, breakfasts, and running the chalet. Cost £285.

Leith's School of Food and Wine
21 St Alban's Grove, London W8 5BP; 071-229 0177
Founded in 1975 by Prue Leith who believes that 'food should make you hungry, not impress you with its ornateness', the Leith School trains cooks for work in catering firms, directors' dining rooms, restaurants, the testing of food products, television commercials and cookery or wine journalism. The school maintains close contact with employers in order to help graduates find jobs. It is non-residential, and no entry qualifications are required. Entry is by interview. The fees range from £6,280 (diploma course) to £270 for a week's course including VAT.

Leith's Diploma in Food and Wine, nine months
There are three exams: written, practical, and a higher certificate examination in wine. Visits are made to markets at New
Smithfield and New Covent Garden, and about three hours a
week are spent on homework – doing such things as menu-
planning, costing, ordering and working on projects.

Beginners' Certificate in Food and Wine, 10 weeks
A course to teach family cooking, both French and English, to
beginners. There are elementary examinations to obtain the
certificate.

Intermediate Certificate in Food and Wine, 11 weeks
A course for those with a sound basic knowledge of cookery. It
follows the same lines as the certificate for beginners but
proceeds at a faster pace. There is an examination.

Advanced Certificate in Food and Wine, 11 weeks
A course for the accomplished cook which includes bisques,
seafood, aspic, French breads etc, as well as cooking for the film
industry, business management and accounts, recipe writing
and meat buying. There are examinations including the higher
wine certificate.

Introduction to Restaurant Management
A new, popular spring course of 10 evening classes in running
your own restaurant.

Other Courses
Leith's also run a series of holiday one-week and four-week
courses between July and September, and evening classes for the
cook/hostess. There are also evening courses leading to the
certificate, higher certificate and advanced certificate in wine.
Note that Leith's courses get booked up a year ahead.

The Manor School of Fine Cuisine
Old Melton Road, Widmerpool, Nottinghamshire NG12 5QL; 0949
81371

*Certificate Course; intensive four-week course. £889
(non-residents) and £989 (residents)*
Tailored for those who want to gain a recognised qualification
and want a career within the culinary profession. Course covers

basic methods, more advanced practical and creative skills, with a good knowledge of cordon bleu cuisine and professional skills. A graded certificate is awarded on successful completion of the course, and a letter of recommendation if the student is sufficiently competent to use the training in a possible future career.

Short courses include vegetarian cuisine, new English cooking.

Tante Marie School of Cookery
Woodham House, Carlton Road, Woking, Surrey GU21 4HF; 04862 26957
The Tante Marie School offers non-residential courses.

Cordon Bleu Certificate Course, 12 weeks
Starting in January, April and September, this course is open to anyone aged 16 and over. Practical classes, demonstrations, and one lecture a week make up the programme. This is a popular course for pre-university year students.

Cordon Bleu Diploma Course, three terms
This is a course starting in September that includes both English and French cookery with a Wine and Spirit Education Trust Certificate course and some flower arranging. Intermediate exams are held in the spring and the final exam is held in the summer. Minimum entry age is 16.

Intensive Cordon Bleu Course, two terms
Applicants for this course must be 18, have prior experience of cookery and be able to maintain the pace set for the course. The same exams are taken as for the diploma course.

Job Opportunities
Tante Marie trained cooks often work in directors' dining rooms and small exclusive hotels, as food stylists, for politicians and TV personalities, in chalets in skiing resorts; some set up their own catering concerns. The Employment Department's Career Development Loans can help students to pay for training.

Short Courses and Demonstrations
Courses include fish cookery, French pâtisserie and cooking for entertaining. One-day demonstrations are held throughout the year.

Costs for 1993 are Diploma course £1,950 per term; Intensive

Diploma course £2,300 per term, and Certificate course £2,400 per term, inclusive of VAT.

The Vegetarian Society
Parkdale, Dunham Road, Altrincham, Cheshire WA14 4QG; 061-928 0793

Cordon Vert Diploma
Four courses: Foundation 1, 2, 3 and 4, each one week long and taken in sequence over a period of time to suit the student. Course content includes familiarisation and practical use of wholefood from readily available to more unusual ingredients such as shoyu, miso, arame, tamari and carob syrup; wholefood adaptation of conventional cookery techniques and dietary and menu planning advice for nutritionally sound meals. Foundation 1, 2 and 3, non-residential, £235; Foundation 4, £260.

Professional Cordon Vert Diploma
Three separate two-day courses at levels 1, 2 and 3, for those already in the catering industry only. From June 1993 the course is more intensive and consists of two levels, each lasting two and a half days. Non-residential, £315.

So You Want to Open Your Own Vegetarian Restaurant?
Weekend course; non-residential, £160.

Learning to Demonstrate
Weekend course for those who want to run their own courses (such as evening classes) or present vegetarian food demonstrations; intended for cooks who have already completed a Parkdale course and are vegetarians themselves. Non-residential, £160.

Other short courses include Italian Vegetarian Cookery, £140.

Chapter 12

Catering College Courses

There are many different colleges and different courses in the country. Normally school-leavers are encouraged to go to their local college, as local education grants may be awarded for local courses. The following courses are held in various colleges as keyed below. See also Chapter 9 for higher level courses.
* Colleges offering Leisure and Tourism/Hospitality.

Key number

Food Preparation and Cooking

Level 1	1
Level 2	2
Level 3	3
Level 4	4

Serving Food and Drink

Level 1	5
Level 2	6

Food and Drink Service

Level 3	7
Level 4	8

Reception and Portering

Level 1	9

Reception

Level 2	10
Level 3	11
Level 4	12

Housekeeping

Level 1	13
Level 3	14
Level 4	15

Guest Service

Level 1	16

BTEC/SCOTVEC

First Certificate	17
First Diploma	18
National Certificate	19
National Diploma	20
Higher National Certificate (HNC)	21
Higher National Diploma (HND)	22

HCIMA

Professional Certificate	23
Professional Diploma	24

England

Avon
City of Bath College,* Avon Street, Bath BA1 1UP
1, 2, 3, 5, 6, 7, 9, 11, 13, 19, 20
Brunel College,* Ashley Down, Bristol BS7 9BU
1, 2, 3, 5, 6, 7, 8, 9, 10, 11, 12,13, 14, 15, 18, 20, 22, 23, 24
Weston-super-Mare College of FE, Knightstone Road, Weston-super-Mare BS23 2AL
1, 2, 18, 20

Bedfordshire
Barnfield College, New Bedford Road, Luton LU3 2AX
1, 2, 3, 5, 6, 7, 9, 10, 11, 19, 20, 21, 22, 23
Bedford College of HE,* School of Social Service Studies, Cauldwell Street, Bedford MK42 9AH
1, 2, 5, 6, 9, 18, 20

Berkshire
Bracknell College, Church Road, Bracknell RG12 1DJ
1, 2, 3, 5, 6, 9, 10, 11, 16
Newbury College of FE, Oxford Road, Newbury RG13 1PQ
1, 2, 5, 6, 17

Reading College, Crescent Road, Reading RG1 5RQ
1, 2, 3, 5, 6, 7, 18, 20, 22
Thames Valley University, Wellington Street, Slough SL1 1YG
1, 2, 3, 4, 5, 6, 7, 8, 9, 10, 11, 12, 13, 14, 15, 19, 20, 21, 22, 23, 24

Buckinghamshire
Aylesbury College, Oxford Road, Aylesbury HP21 8PD
1, 2, 5, 6, 9, 10, 13, 18, 20, 23
Milton Keynes College, Bletchley Centre, Sherwood Drive, Bletchley, Milton Keynes MK3 6DR
1, 2, 3, 4, 5, 6, 9, 10, 20, 23

Cambridgeshire
Cambridge Regional College,* Newmarket Road, Cambridge CB5 8EG
1, 2, 3, 5, 6, 10, 11, 13, 18, 20, 23
Peterborough Regional College, Park Crescent, Peterborough PE1 4DZ
1, 2, 3, 5, 6, 7, 18, 20

Cheshire
Halton College of FE,* Kingsway, Widnes WA8 7QQ
1, 2, 3, 5, 6, 7, 9, 10, 11, 18, 20
Macclesfield College of FE, Park Lane, Macclesfield SK11 8LF
Apply to College.
Mid-Cheshire College of FE, Hartford Campus, Northwich CW8 1LJ
1, 2, 3, 5, 6, 7, 9, 10, 11, 16, 18, 20
South Cheshire College, Dane Bank Avenue, Crewe CW2 8AB
1, 2, 3, 5, 6, 7, 17, 18, 19, 20, 23
West Cheshire College, Greenbank Centre, Eaton Road, Handbridge, Chester CH4 7ER
1, 2, 5, 6, 9, 10, 11, 16, 20

Cleveland
Kirby College,* Roman Road, Middlesbrough TS5 5PJ
1, 2, 3, 5, 6, 7, 9, 10, 11, 19, 20

Cornwall
Cornwall College,* Pool, Redruth TR15 3RD
2, 6, 20, 23
St Austell College, Palace Road, St Austell PL25 4BW
1, 2, 5, 6

Cumbria
Carlisle College,* Victoria Place, Carlisle CA1 1HS
1, 2, 3, 4, 5, 6, 7, 8, 9, 10, 11, 12, 13, 14, 15, 17, 18, 19, 20
Kendal College of FE, Milnthorpe Road, Kendal LA9 5AY
1, 2, 3, 4, 5, 6, 7, 8, 9, 10, 11, 12, 20, 23

West Cumbria College,* Park Lane, Workington CA14 2RW
1, 2, 3, 4, 5, 6, 7, 8, 9, 10, 11, 12, 18, 20
Furness College,* Howard Street, Barrow in Furness LA14 4JS
1, 2, 5, 6, 18

Derbyshire
Chesterfield College of Technology and Arts,* Infirmary Road, Chesterfield S41 7NG
1, 2, 3, 5, 6, 7, 9, 10, 11, 13, 14, 17, 20
Derby Tertiary College, London Road, Wilmorton, Derby DE24 8UG
1, 2, 3, 5, 6, 7, 9, 10, 11, 13, 14, 16, 20
High Peak College,* Harpur Hill, Buxton SK17 9JZ
1, 2, 6, 7, 9, 10, 11, 14
North Derbyshire Tertiary College, Rectory Road, Clowne, Chesterfield
S43 4BQ
1, 2, 5

Devon
East Devon College of FE, Bolham Road, Tiverton EX16 6SH
1, 2, 3, 5, 6, 7, 9, 10, 11, 17, 18
Exeter College,* Hele Road, Exeter EX4 4JS
1, 2, 3, 4, 5, 6, 7, 8, 9, 10, 11, 12, 13, 14, 15, 16, 18, 23
North Devon College, Sticklepath Hill, Barnstaple EX31 2BQ
1, 2, 3, 5, 6, 7, 9, 10, 11, 13, 14, 16, 20, 23
Plymouth College of FE, Kings Road, Devonport, Plymouth PL1 5QG
1, 2, 3, 5, 6, 9, 18, 20, 22
South Devon College, Newton Road, Torquay TQ2 5BY
1, 2, 3, 5, 6, 7, 9, 10, 17, 18, 19, 20, 22, 23, 24

Dorset
Bournemouth and Poole College of FE, The Lansdowne, Bournemouth
BH1 3JJ
2, 3, 5, 6, 7, 9, 10, 11, 13, 14, 18, 20, 23
Weymouth College,* Newstead Road, Weymouth DT4 0DX
1, 2, 3, 5, 6, 7, 9, 10, 18, 20

Durham
Darlington College of Technology, Cleveland Avenue, Darlington
DL3 7BB
1, 2, 5, 6, 9, 13, 18, 20
Derwentside College, Park Road, Consett DH8 5EE
1, 2, 5, 6, 9, 13, 16
New College, Framwellgate Moor, Durham DH1 5ES
1, 2, 3, 5, 6, 7, 9, 10, 11, 13, 14, 18, 20
Peterlee College, Peterlee SR8 1NU
1, 2, 3, 5

Essex
Barking College,* Dagenham Road, Romford RM7 0XU
1, 2
Braintree College of FE, Church Lane, Braintree CM7 5SN
1, 2, 3, 4, 5, 6, 7, 8, 18
Chelmsford College of FE, Princes Road, Chelmsford CM2 9DX
1, 2, 5, 6, 20, 23
Colchester Institute, Sheepen Road, Colchester CO3 3LL
1, 2, 3, 5, 6, 7, 9, 10, 14, 16, 18, 19, 20, 22
Harlow College,* College Square, The High, Harlow CM20 1LT
1, 2, 3, 5, 6, 7, 9, 10, 11, 13, 14, 16, 18, 19, 20
Havering College of F&HE, Tring Gardens, Harold Hill, Romford RM3 9ES
1, 2, 3, 5, 6, 7, 17
Redbridge College of FE, Little Heath, Romford RM6 4XT
1, 2, 5, 6
South East Essex College of Arts and Technology, Carnarvon Road, Southend on Sea SS2 6LS
1, 2, 3, 5, 6, 7, 9, 10, 11, 18, 23
Thurrock College,* Woodview, Grays RM16 4YR
1, 2, 3, 5, 6, 7, 9, 10, 11, 13, 14, 16, 20

Gloucestershire
Gloucestershire College of Arts and Technology,* 73 The Park, Cheltenham GL50 2RR
1, 2, 3, 4, 5, 6, 7, 8, 9, 10, 11, 12, 13, 14, 15, 16, 18, 20
The Royal Forest of Dean College, Five Acres Campus, Berry Hill, Coleford GL16 7JT
1, 2, 5, 6

Hampshire and the Isle of Wight
Basingstoke College of Technology, Worting Street, Basingstoke RG21 1TN
1, 2, 3, 5, 6, 7, 20
Brockenhurst College, Lyndhurst Road, Brockenhurst SO42 7ZE
1, 2, 5, 6, 18
Cricklade College, Charlton Road, Andover SP10 1EJ
1, 2, 3, 5, 6, 7, 17
Eastleigh College, Chestnut Avenue, Eastleigh SO5 5HT
1, 2, 3, 5, 6, 7, 9, 10, 13, 18, 20
Fareham College, Bishopsfield Road, Fareham PO14 1NH
1, 2, 5
Farnborough College of Technology, Boundary Road, Farnborough GU14 6SB
1, 2, 3, 5, 6, 7, 16, 20, 22
Highbury College,* Dovercourt Road, Cosham, Portsmouth PO6 2SA
1, 2, 3, 5, 6, 7, 9, 10, 11, 13, 14, 21, 22

Isle of Wight College of Arts and Technology,* Medina Way, Newport
PO30 5TA
1, 2, 3, 5, 6, 7, 9, 10, 11, 17, 18, 19, 20
Southampton Technical College,* St Mary's Street, Southampton
SO9 4WX
1, 2, 3, 4, 5, 6, 7, 9, 16, 19, 20
South Downs College of FE,* College Road, Havant PO7 8AA
1, 2, 3, 5, 6, 7, 9, 10, 11, 13, 14, 16, 17

Hereford and Worcester
Herefordshire College of Technology,* Folly Lane, Hereford HR1 1LS
1, 2, 3, 4, 5, 6, 7, 8, 9, 10, 11, 13, 14, 15, 16, 18, 20, 22
North East Worcestershire College,* Redditch Campus, Peakman
Street, Redditch B98 8DW
1, 2, 3, 4, 5, 6, 7, 8, 13, 17, 18, 20
Worcester College of Technology,* Deansway, Worcester WR1 2JF
2, 5, 6, 7, 9, 10, 11, 13, 14, 17

Hertfordshire
Hertford Regional College, Scotts Road, Ware SG12 9JF
1, 2, 5, 6
North Hertfordshire College, Broadway, Letchworth SG6 3PB
1, 2, 3, 4, 5, 6, 7, 9, 10, 16, 18, 19, 20, 23
West Herts College, Cassio Campus, Langley Road, Watford WD1 3RH
1, 2, 3, 5, 6, 7, 10, 18, 20, 22

Humberside
Beverley College of FE, Gallows Lane, Beverley HU17 7DT
1, 2, 3, 5, 6, 7, 9, 10, 11, 13, 17, 18, 19, 20
East Yorkshire College,* St Mary's Walk, Bridlington YO16 5JW
1, 2, 3, 5, 6, 7, 9, 10, 13, 16
Grimsby College of Technology and Arts,* Nuns' Corner, Grimsby
DN34 5BQ
2, 3, 6, 7, 10, 11, 14, 18, 19, 20, 21, 22
Hull College of FE,* Queens Gardens, Hull HU1 3DG
1, 2, 3, 5, 6, 7, 17, 18, 19, 20, 22, 23
North Lindsey College,* Kingsway, Scunthorpe DN17 1AJ
1, 2, 3, 5, 6, 7, 9, 10, 11, 13, 16, 20

Kent
Canterbury College, New Dover Road, Canterbury CT1 3AJ
1, 2, 4, 5, 6, 7, 9, 10, 14
Mid-Kent College of H&FE,* Oakwood Park, Tonbridge Road, Maidstone
ME16 8AQ
1, 2, 3, 5, 6, 7, 9, 10, 13, 16, 18, 19
North West Kent College of Technology,* Miskin Road, Dartford
DA1 2LU

1, 2, 5, 6, 9, 10, 13, 16, 20, 22
South Kent College, Shorncliffe Road, Folkestone CT20 2NA
1, 2, 3, 5, 6, 7, 9, 10, 11, 16, 18
Thanet Technical College, Ramsgate Road, Broadstairs CT10 1PN
1, 2, 3, 5, 6, 7, 9, 10, 13, 16, 18, 20, 22
West Kent College, Brook Street, Tonbridge TN9 2PW
1, 2, 3, 5, 6, 7, 9, 10, 11, 13, 14, 16, 18, 19, 20, 23

Lancashire and Isle of Man
Accrington and Rossendale College,* Blackburn Road, Accrington BB5 0AQ
1, 2, 3, 5, 6, 7, 16, 17, 18, 21, 22
Blackburn College, Feilden Street, Blackburn BB2 1LH
1, 2, 3, 5, 6, 7, 9, 13, 16, 18, 20
Blackpool and The Fylde College, Park Road, Blackpool FY1 4JN
1, 2, 3, 4, 5, 6, 7, 8, 17, 18
  School of Hospitality, Food and Management,* Ashfield Road, Bispham, Blackpool FY2 0HB
1, 2, 3, 4, 5, 6, 7, 8, 9, 10, 18, 20, 21, 22
Isle of Man College, Homefield Road, Douglas
1, 2, 3, 5, 6, 7, 17, 18, 19, 20
Lancaster and Morecambe College, Morecambe Road, Lancaster LA1 2TY
1, 2, 3, 5, 6, 7, 9, 10, 13, 16, 20
Leigh College, Railway Road, Leigh
1, 2, 6, 20
Nelson and Colne College, Scotland Road, Nelson BB9 7YT
1, 2, 5, 6, 17, 18, 19, 20
Preston College,* St Vincent Road, Fulwood, Preston PR2 4UR
1, 2, 3, 4, 5, 6, 7, 8, 17, 18, 19, 20
Runshaw College, School of Catering, Langdale Road, Leyland PR5 2DQ
1, 2, 3, 5, 6, 7, 10, 17, 18, 19, 20
Wigan and Leigh College, Parson's Walk, Wigan WN1 1RS
1, 2, 3, 5, 6, 7, 13, 18, 20

Leicestershire
Coalville Technical College, Bridge Road, Coalville LE6 2QR
1, 2, 5, 6, 10, 13, 16
Hinckley College of FE, London Road, Hinckley LE10 1XR
1, 2, 5, 6, 16, 17, 18
Loughborough College, Radmoor, Loughborough LE11 3BT
2, 3, 6, 7, 10, 11, 13, 18, 20
Melton Mowbray College of FE, Asfordby Road, Melton Mowbray LE13 0HJ
Apply to College
South Fields College of FE,* Aylestone Road, Leicester LE2 7LW
1, 2, 3, 5, 6, 7, 17, 18, 19, 20, 22

Lincolnshire
Boston College of FE, Rowley Road, Boston PE21 6JF
1, 2, 3, 5, 6, 7, 16, 18, 20
Grantham College,* Stonebridge Road, Grantham NG31 9AP
1, 2, 5, 6
North Lincolnshire College,* Cathedral Street, Lincoln LN1 5HQ
1, 2, 3, 4, 5, 6, 7, 8, 9, 10, 11, 12, 13, 14, 15, 18, 19, 20, 23
Stamford College,* Melborne Road, Stamford PE9 1XA
1, 2, 3, 5, 6, 7, 9, 10, 11, 13, 14, 18, 20

London
Barnet College of FE, Russell Lane, London N20 0AX
Apply to College
College of North West London (Brent), Priory Park Road, London
NW6 7UJ
1, 2, 5, 6
Hendon College, Corner Mead, Grahame Park Way, London NW9 5RA
1, 2, 3, 5, 6, 7, 17, 20, 22
Hounslow Borough College,* London Road, Isleworth, Middlesex
TW7 4HS
1, 2, 3, 5, 6, 7, 9, 10, 11, 13, 14, 16, 19, 20
Lewisham College, Breakspears Road, Lewisham Way, London SE4 1UT
1, 2, 5, 6, 20, 23
Merton College,* London Road, Morden, Surrey SM4 5QX
1, 2, 3, 5, 6, 7, 19, 20
Newham Community College, Welfare Road, Stratford, London E15 4HT
1, 2, 3, 17
Richmond upon Thames Tertiary College, Egerton Road, Twickenham,
Middlesex TW2 7SJ
Apply to College
Southgate College, High Street, London N14 6BS
1, 2, 3, 5, 6, 7, 18, 19, 20, 21
Thames Valley University,* St Mary's Road, Ealing, London W5 5RF
2, 3, 4, 6, 7, 8, 10, 11, 12, 20, 21, 22, 23
Uxbridge College, Park Road, Uxbridge UB8 1NQ
1, 2, 5, 6
Waltham Forest College,* Forest Road, London E17 4JB
1, 2, 3, 5, 6, 7, 9, 10, 11, 13, 14, 16, 18, 19, 20
Weald College, Brookshill, Harrow Weald, Middlesex HA3 6RR
1, 2, 5, 6, 17, 18
Westminster College, Vincent Square, London SW1P 2PD *and* Battersea
Park Road, London SW11 4JR
1, 2, 3, 4, 5, 6, 7, 8, 9, 10, 11, 12, 13, 14, 15, 16, 18, 20, 21, 22, 23, 24

Greater Manchester
Bolton Metropolitan College,* Manchester Road, Bolton BL2 1ER
1, 2, 3, 4, 5, 6, 7, 8, 9, 10, 11, 12, 13, 14, 15, 16, 20, 23

Bury College, Whitfield Centre, Albert Road, Whitfield, Bury M25 5NH
1, 2, 3, 5, 6, 10, 17, 19, 20, 23
Hopwood Hall Tertiary College, St Mary's Gate Campus, Rochdale
OL12 6RY
1, 2, 3, 5, 6, 7, 18, 20
Manchester College of Arts and Technology,* City Centre Campus,
Lower Hardman Street, Manchester M3 3ER
 Moston Campus, Ashley Lane, Moston, Manchester M9 1WU
 Openshaw Campus, Whitworth Street, Openshaw, Manchester
M11 2WH
1, 2, 5, 6, 18, 20
Oldham College,* Rochdale Road, Oldham OL9 6AA
1, 2, 5, 6, 18, 19, 20
South Manchester College, Fielden Park Centre, 141 Barlow Moor Road,
West Didsbury, Manchester M20 8PQ
1,2, 3, 5, 6, 7, 9, 10, 13, 17, 19
South Trafford College, Manchester Road, West Timperley, Altrincham
WA14 5PQ
1, 2, 3, 6, 7, 20
Tameside College of Technology, Beaufort Road, Ashton-under-Lyne
OL6 6NX
1, 2, 5, 6, 9, 10, 13, 16, 17, 20, 23
University College Salford, Frederick Road, Salford M6 6PU
1, 2, 3, 4, 5, 6, 7, 8, 13, 14, 15, 19, 20, 22, 23

Merseyside
City of Liverpool Community College, Colquitt Centre, Liverpool L1 4DB
1, 2, 3, 5, 6, 13, 20
Hugh Baird College, Church Road, Litherland L21 5HA
1, 2, 5, 6, 18
Knowsley Community College, Rupert Road, Huyton, Roby L36 9TD
1, 2, 5, 6, 18, 19
St Helens Community College,* Brook Street, St Helens WA10 1PZ
1, 2, 3, 4, 5, 6, 7, 8, 9, 10, 13, 18, 20, 21
Southport College,* Mornington Road, Southport PR9 0TT
1, 2, 3, 5, 6, 7, 9, 10, 13, 20
Wirral Metropolitan College, Borough Road, Birkenhead L42 9QD
1, 2, 3, 5, 6, 7
Wirral Metropolitan College,* Carlett Park, Eastham L62 0AY
1, 2, 3, 4, 5, 6, 7, 8, 10, 11, 13, 14, 17, 18, 19, 21, 22, 23, 24

Norfolk
Great Yarmouth College of FE, Southtown, Great Yarmouth NR31 0ED
1, 2, 3, 5, 6, 7, 9, 10, 16
Norfolk College of Arts and Technology, Tennyson Avenue, Kings Lynn
PE30 2QW
1, 2, 5, 6, 9, 10, 13, 16

Norwich City College of F&HE,* Ipswich Road, Norwich NR2 2LJ
1, 2, 3, 5, 6, 7, 9, 22, 23

Northamptonshire
Northampton College, Booth Lane South, Northampton NN3 3RF
1, 2, 3, 6, 7, 10, 18, 19, 20
Tresham Institute, George Street, Corby NN17 1QA
1, 2, 3, 5, 6, 7, 18, 20

Northumberland
Northumberland College of Arts and Technology, College Road, Ashington NE63 9RG
1, 2, 3, 5, 6, 7, 9, 10, 11, 13, 16, 17, 18, 20

Nottinghamshire
Clarendon College, Pelham Avenue, Nottingham NG5 1AL
1, 2, 3, 4, 5, 6, 7, 8, 9, 10, 13, 16, 17, 18, 19, 20, 21, 22, 23, 24
North Nottinghamshire College of FE, Carlton Road, Worksop S81 7HP
1, 2, 5, 6, 10
West Nottinghamshire College,* Derby Road, Mansfield NG18 5BH
1, 2, 3, 5, 6, 7, 9, 10, 11, 13, 16, 18, 20

Oxfordshire
Abingdon College, Northcourt Road, Abingdon OX14 1NN
1, 2, 5, 6
Henley College, Deanfield Avenue, Henley on Thames RG9 1UH
1, 2, 5, 6, 18
North Oxfordshire College and School of Art, Broughton Road, Banbury OX16 9QA
1, 2, 3, 5, 6, 7, 16, 17, 18
Oxford College of FE,* Oxpens Road, Oxford OX1 1SA
1, 2, 3, 5, 6, 7, 9, 10, 13, 16, 18, 19, 23, 24

Shropshire
Shrewsbury College of Arts and Technology, Radbrook Centre, Radbrook Road, Shrewsbury SY3 9BL
1, 2, 5, 6, 17, 18, 19, 20
Telford College of Arts and Technology, Haybridge Road, Wellington, Telford TF1 2NP
1, 2, 3, 5, 6

Somerset
Somerset College of Arts and Technology, Wellington Road, Taunton TA1 5AX
1, 2, 3, 5, 6, 7, 9, 18, 19, 20
Yeovil College, Ilchester Road, Yeovil BA21 3BA
Apply to College

Staffordshire
Burton upon Trent Technical College, Lichfield Street, Burton upon Trent DE14 3RL
1, 2, 3, 4, 5, 6, 7, 8, 9, 10, 13, 16, 17, 18, 20, 23
Cannock Chase Technical College, The Green, Cannock WS11 1UE
1, 2, 5, 6, 13, 17, 18
Newcastle-under-Lyme College, Liverpool Road, Newcastle-under-Lyme ST5 2DG
Apply to College
Stafford College, Earl Street, Stafford ST16 2QR
1, 2, 3, 5, 6, 7, 9, 10, 13, 17, 18, 20, 21, 22
Stoke-on-Trent College,* Cauldon Campus, Stoke Road, Shelton, Stoke-on-Trent ST4 2DG
1, 2, 3, 5, 6, 7, 9, 10, 13, 18, 20, 22
Tamworth College, Croft Street, Upper Gungate, Tamworth B79 8AE
1, 2, 3, 5, 6, 7, 18, 20

Suffolk
Lowestoft College,* St Peter's Street, Lowestoft NR32 2NB
1, 2, 3, 5, 6, 7, 9, 10, 11, 20
Suffolk College of H&FE, Rope Walk, Ipswich IP4 1LT
1, 2, 3, 5, 6, 7, 9, 10
West Suffolk College, Out Risbygate, Bury St Edmunds IP33 3RL
1, 2, 3, 5, 6, 7, 9, 10, 13, 18, 19, 20, 23

Surrey
Brooklands College, Heath Road, Weybridge KT13 8TT
1, 2, 3, 5, 6, 7, 9, 10, 11, 13, 14, 16, 18, 20
Carshalton College,* Nightingale Road, Carshalton SM5 2EU
1, 2, 3, 5, 6, 7, 9, 10, 11, 13, 16, 18, 20
Croydon College, Fairfield, Croydon CR9 1DX
1, 2, 3, 4, 5, 6, 7, 18, 20, 22, 23
Guildford College,* Stoke Park, Guildford GU1 1EZ
1, 2, 3, 4, 5, 6, 7, 8, 9, 10, 11, 13, 14, 18, 20, 22
North East Surrey College of Technology, Reigate Road, Ewell KT17 3DS
Apply to College

Sussex (East)
Brighton College of Technology, Pelham Street, Brighton BN1 4FA
1, 2, 3, 5, 6, 7, 9, 10, 13, 16, 19, 22, 23, 24
Eastbourne College of Arts and Technology, Kings Drive, Eastbourne BN21 2UN
1, 2, 3, 5, 6, 7, 10, 13, 20
Hastings College of Arts and Technology,* St Leonards-on-Sea TN38 0HX
1, 2, 3, 5, 6, 7, 9, 10, 16, 17, 18, 20

Sussex (West)
Chichester College of Technology,* Westgate Fields, Chichester
PO19 1SB
1, 2, 3, 5, 7, 10, 17, 18, 19, 20
Crawley College,* College Road, Crawley RH10 1NR
1, 2, 3, 5, 6, 7, 9, 10, 13, 16, 17, 18, 20, 23
Northbrook College of Design and Technology,* Littlehampton Road,
Goring by Sea BN12 6NV
1, 2, 3, 5, 6, 7, 10, 18, 20

Tyne and Wear
Monkwearmouth College,* Swan Street Centre, Sunderland SR5 1EB
1, 2, 3, 5, 6, 7, 9, 10, 11, 13, 14, 16, 18, 20, 22
Newcastle College,* Sandyford Road, Newcastle upon Tyne NE1 8QE
1, 2, 3, 4, 5, 6, 7, 8, 17, 18, 19, 20, 22, 23, 24
North Tyneside College, Embleton Avenue, Wallsend NE28 9NJ
1, 2, 5, 6, 9, 10, 13, 16, 20
South Tyneside College, St George's Avenue, South Shields NE34 6ET
1, 2, 5, 6, 18, 19, 20

Warwickshire
East Warwickshire College of FE,* Lower Hillmorton Road, Rugby
CV21 3QS
1, 2, 3, 5, 6, 7, 17
North Warwickshire College, Hinckley Road, Nuneaton CV11 6BH
1, 2, 3, 5, 6, 7, 9, 10, 11, 13, 14, 16, 17, 18, 19, 20
Stratford-upon-Avon College, The Willows North, Alcester Road,
Stratford-on-Avon CV37 9QR
1, 2, 3, 5, 6, 7, 9, 10, 11, 13, 16, 17, 18, 19, 20

West Midlands
Bilston Community College, Westfield Road, Bilston, Wolverhampton
WV14 6ER
1, 2, 6
Birmingham College of Food, Tourism and Creative Studies, Summer
Row, Birmingham B3 1JB
1, 2, 3, 4, 5, 6, 7, 8, 9, 10, 11, 20, 21, 22
Bournville College of FE, Bristol Road South, Birmingham B31 2AJ
1, 2, 3, 5, 6, 7
East Birmingham College, Garretts Green Lane, Sheldon, Birmingham
B33 0TS
1, 2, 3, 4, 5, 6, 7, 8, 17, 18
Halesowen College, Whittingham Road, Halesowen B63 3NA
1, 2, 3, 5, 6, 7, 9, 10, 11, 13, 14, 17, 18, 19, 20, 23
Handsworth College of F&HE, The Council, Soho Road, Handsworth,
Birmingham B15 3PH
1, 2, 5

Henley College Coventry, Henley Road, Bell Green, Coventry CV2 1ED
1, 2, 3, 4, 5, 6, 18, 20, 22, 23, 24
Sandwell College of F&HE, High Street, West Bromwich B70 8DW
1, 2, 3, 5, 6, 7, 9, 10, 11, 13, 14, 17, 18, 19, 20
Solihull College of Technology, Blossomfield Road, Solihull B91 1SB
1, 2, 3, 5, 6, 7, 9, 10, 11, 18, 19, 20
Sutton College of FE, Lichfield Road, Sutton Coldfield B74 2NW
1, 2, 3, 5, 6, 7, 18, 20
University of Wolverhampton, Compton Road West, Compton Park,
Wolverhampton WV3 9DX
4, 8, 22
Walsall College of Arts and Technology,* St Paul's Street, Walsall
WS1 1XN
1, 2, 3, 4, 5, 6, 7, 8, 9, 10, 11, 13, 16, 17, 18, 19, 20, 21, 22

Wiltshire
Chippenham Technical College, Cocklebury Road, Chippenham
SN15 3QD
2, 11
Salisbury College, Southampton Road, Salisbury SP1 2LW
1, 2, 3, 5, 6, 7, 20
Swindon College,* North Star Avenue, Swindon SN2 1DY
1, 2, 3, 5, 6, 7, 9, 10, 13, 16, 20
Trowbridge College, College Road, Trowbridge BA14 0ES
1, 2, 3, 5, 6, 7

North Yorkshire
Craven College, High Street, Skipton BD23 1JY
1, 2, 3, 5, 6, 7, 20
Harrogate College of Arts and Technology,* Hornbeam Park, Hookstone
Road, Harrogate HG2 8QT
1, 2, 3, 5, 6, 18, 20
Selby College,* Abbot's Road, Selby YO8 8AT
1, 2, 3, 5, 6, 7, 10, 17, 18, 20
York College of F&HE, Tadcaster Road, York YO2 1UA
1, 2, 6, 7, 9, 10, 11, 14
Yorkshire Coast College,* Lady Edith's Drive, Scalby Road, Scarborough
YO12 5RN
1, 2, 3, 4, 5, 6, 7, 8, 9, 10, 11, 12, 13, 14, 16, 19, 20, 22

South Yorkshire
Barnsley College,* Church Street, Barnsley S70 2AX
1, 2, 3, 4, 5, 6, 7, 8, 17, 18, 19, 20, 21, 22, 23, 24
Doncaster College,* Waterdale, Doncaster DN1 3EX
1, 2, 3, 5, 6, 7, 20

Rockingham College of FE,* West Street, Wath upon Dearne, Rotherham S63 6PX
1, 2, 3, 5, 6, 7
Rother Valley College, Doe Quarry Lane, Dinnington, Sheffield S31 8QH
1, 2
Rotherham College of Arts and Technology, Eastwood Lane, Rotherham
S65 1EG
1, 2, 3, 5, 6, 20, 21
Sheffield College,* Castle Centre, Granville Road, Sheffield S2 2RL
1, 2, 3, 4, 5, 6, 7, 8, 9, 10, 11, 13, 14, 16, 17, 18, 19, 20, 23

West Yorkshire

Bradford and Ilkley Community College, Great Horton Road, Bradford
BD7 1AY
1, 2, 3, 5, 6, 7, 20, 22
Calderdale College,* E Floor, Percival Whitley Centre, Francis Street,
Halifax HX1 3UZ
1, 2, 5, 6, 16, 18, 20
Dewsbury College, Halifax Road, Dewsbury WF13 2AS
1, 2, 5, 6
Huddersfield Technical College, New North Road, Huddersfield
HD1 5NN
1, 2, 3, 5, 6, 7, 9, 10, 11, 13, 14, 17, 18, 19, 20
Thomas Danby College,* Roundhay Road, Sheepscar, Leeds LS37 3BG
1, 2, 3, 4, 5, 6, 7, 8, 9, 10, 11, 13, 14, 18, 20, 23
Wakefield College,* Margaret Street, Wakefield WF1 2DH
1, 2, 3, 5, 6, 7, 9, 10, 11, 13, 14, 16, 17, 19, 20, 21, 22

Channel Islands

Guernsey
Guernsey College of Further Education,* Route des Coutanchez, St
Peter Port
1, 2, 3, 5, 6, 7, 9, 10

Jersey
Highlands College,* Box 1000, St Saviour JE4 9QA
1, 2, 3, 4, 5, 6, 7, 8, 9, 10, 11, 12, 13, 14, 15, 16, 18, 19, 20

Isle of Man

Isle of Man College, Homefield Road, Douglas
1, 2, 3, 5, 6, 7, 17, 18, 19, 20

Wales

Clwyd
Deeside College of FE, Kelsterton Road, Connah's Quay
1, 2, 6, 7, 11
Llandrillo College, Llandudno Road, Rhos-on-Sea, Colwyn Bay LL28 4HZ
1, 2, 4, 6, 7, 11, 14, 15, 17, 18, 19

Dyfed
Carmarthenshire College of Technology & Art,* Pibwrlwyd Campus, Carmarthen SA31 2NH
1, 2, 3, 5, 6, 7, 9, 10, 13, 16, 17, 18, 19, 20
Coleg Ceredigon, Plas Tan y Bwlch, Rhdyfelin, Aberystwyth SY23 3PB
1, 2, 3, 5, 6, 7, 9, 13, 16
Coleg Ceredigon, Park Place, Cardigan SA43 1AB
1, 2, 3, 5, 6, 7, 9, 13
Pembrokeshire College, College Campus, Aberdare CF44 8ST
1, 2, 5, 6, 18, 19, 20

Glamorgan
Aberdare College, Cwmdare Hill, Aberdare CF44 8ST
1, 2, 3, 5, 6, 7, 9, 10, 11, 13, 14, 16, 17, 18, 20
Barry College, Colcot Road, Barry CF6 8YJ
1, 2, 3, 5, 6, 7, 10, 11, 13, 17, 18, 20
Bridgend College of Technology, Cowbridge Road, Bridgend CF31 3DF
1, 2, 5, 6, 18, 20
Cardiff Institute of HE, Colchester Road, Cardiff CF3 7XR
1, 2, 5, 6, 17, 18, 19, 20, 21, 22
Merthyr Tydfil College, Ynysfach, Merthyr Tydfil CF48 1AR
1, 2, 5, 6, 17, 18, 19, 20
Neath College, Dwr-y-Felin Road, Neath SA10 7RF
1, 2, 5, 6, 9, 10, 13, 16, 18, 19, 20
Pontypridd Technical College, Ynys Terrace, Rhydyfelin CF37 5RN
1, 2, 5, 6
Rhondda College of FE,* Llwynypi, Tonypandy CF40 2TQ
1, 2, 3, 5, 6, 7, 9, 10, 11, 13, 14, 16, 17, 18, 19, 20
Swansea College, Tycoch Road, Sketty, Swansea SA2 9EB
1, 2, 3, 5, 6, 7, 9, 10, 13, 16, 18, 19, 20
Ystrad Mynach College, Twyn Road, Hengoed, Ystrad Mynach CF8 7XR
1, 2, 5, 6, 17, 18, 19, 20

Gwent
Gwent Tertiary College,* Crosskeys Campus, Risca Road, Crosskeys NP1 7ZA
1, 2, 5, 6, 17, 18

Gwent Tertiary College, Ebbw Vale Campus, College Road, Ebbw Vale NP3 6LE
1, 2, 3, 5, 6, 7
Gwent Tertiary College,* Newport Campus, Nash Road, Newport NP9 0TS
1, 2, 3, 5, 6, 13, 20
Gwent Tertiary College, Pontypool and Usk College Campus, Twmpath Annexe, Tympath Road, Pontypool NP4 6AQ
1, 2, 3, 5, 6, 7, 10, 17, 18, 19, 20

Gwynedd
Coleg Meirion Dwyfor,* Barmouth Road, Dolgellau LL40 2SW
1, 2, 3, 5, 6, 7, 10, 17, 18, 19, 20
Gwynedd Technical College,* Ffriddoedd Road, Bangor LL57 2TP
1, 2, 3, 4, 5, 6, 7, 8, 9, 10, 11, 13, 14, 16, 18, 19, 20
Coleg Pencraig, Ynys Mon, Llangefni LL77 7HY
1, 2, 3, 5, 6, 7, 18

Powys
Coleg Powys Brecon,* Penlan, Brecon LD3 9SR
1, 2, 3, 5, 6
Coleg Powys Montgomery Coleg Site, Llanidloes Road, Newtown SY16 1BE
1, 2, 3, 5, 6, 7, 9, 13, 17, 18, 19, 20

Scotland

Borders
Borders College,* Henderson Building, Commercial Road, Hawick TD9 7AW
19, 21, 23

Central
Clackmannan College of FE,* Branshill Road, Alloa FK10 3BT
19
Falkirk College,* Grangemouth Road, Falkirk FK2 9AD
19, 21

Dumfries and Galloway
Dumfries and Galloway College of Technology,* Heathhall, Dumfries DG1 3QZ
1, 2, 3, 5, 6, 19, 21, 22, 23

Fife
Elmwood College, Carslogie Road, Cupar KY15 4SB
1, 2, 5, 6, 19, 21

Fife College of Technology,* St Brycedale Avenue, Kirkcaldy KY1 1EX
1, 2, 3, 5, 6, 7, 19, 21, 22
Glenrothes College, Stenton Road, Glenrothes KY6 2RA
19
Lauder College,* Halbeath, Dunfermline KY11 5DY
19, 21, 22, 23

Grampian
Aberdeen College of FE, Gallowgate, Aberdeen AB9 1DN
1, 2, 3, 4, 5, 6, 7, 8, 9, 10, 11, 12, 13, 14, 15, 16, 19, 21, 22, 23
Banff and Buchan College of FE, Henderson Road, Fraserburgh
AB43 5GA
1, 2, 3, 5, 6, 7, 13, 14, 19
Moray College of FE,* Hay Street, Elgin IV30 1NQ
1, 2, 3, 5, 6, 7, 9, 10, 11, 13, 14, 16, 21

Highland
Inverness College,* 3 Longman Road, Inverness IV1 1SA
1, 2, 3, 5, 6, 7, 9, 10, 11, 13, 14, 16, 19, 21, 23
Thurso College,* Ormlie Road, Thurso KW14 7EE
1, 2, 3, 5, 6, 7, 9, 10, 13, 14, 16, 19, 23

Lothian
Jewel and Esk Valley College,* Eskbank Centre, Newbattle Road,
Dalkeith EH22 3AE
2, 6, 19, 21
Telford College of FE,* Crewe Toll, Edinburgh EH4 2NZ
1, 2, 3, 4, 5, 6, 7, 8, 9, 10, 12, 13, 15, 19, 21, 22, 23
West Lothian College of FE, Marjoribanks Street, Bathgate EH48 1QJ
19

Strathclyde
Ayr College,* Dam Park, Ayr KA8 0EU
1, 2, 3, 5, 6, 7, 19, 21, 22
Cambuslang College,* East Kilbride Annexe, Main Street, East Kilbride
G74 4JZ
21
Clydebank College,* Kilbowie Road, Clydebank G81 2AA
1, 2, 3, 4, 5, 6, 9, 10, 11, 13, 14, 19, 21
Cumbernauld College,* Tryst Road, Town Centre, Cumbernauld
HG67 1HU
19, 21
Glasgow College of Food Technology,* 230 Cathedral Street, Glasgow
G1 2TG
1, 2, 3, 4, 12, 14, 15, 17, 18
James Watt College,* Finnart Street, Greenock PA16 8HF
2, 6, 19, 21, 22

John Wheatley College, 1346 Shettleston Road, Glasgow G32 9AT
1, 2, 5, 6, 19
Kilmarnock College, Bank Street Campus, Irvine KA12 0LP
19
Motherwell College,* Dalzell Drive, Motherwell ML1 2DD
19, 21, 22, 23
Reid Kerr College,* Renfrew Road, Paisley PA3 4DR
1, 2, 3, 4, 5, 6, 7, 8, 9, 10, 11, 12, 13, 14, 19, 21, 22

Tayside
Angus College of FE,* Keptie Road, Arbroath DD11 3EA
19
Duncan of Jordanstone College, Perth Road, Dundee DD1 4HT
21
Dundee College of FE,* Old Glamis Road, Dundee DD3 8LE
1, 2, 3, 5, 6, 7, 19, 21
Perth College of FE,* Brahan Estate, Crieff Road, Perth PH1 2NX
1, 2, 3, 5, 6, 7, 19, 21, 22

Orkney
Kirkwall College of FE, Kirkwall KW15 1QM
1, 2, 5, 6, 19

Shetland
Shetland College of FE,* Gressy Loan, Lerwick ZE1 0BB
1, 2, 5, 6, 19

Western Isles
Lews Castle College,* Stornoway PA86 0XR
1, 2, 3, 5, 6, 7, 9, 10, 11, 13, 14, 16, 19, 21

Northern Ireland

Belfast
Belfast Institute of F&HE, Brunswick Street, Belfast BT2 7GX
1, 2, 3, 5, 6, 7, 9, 10, 19, 20, 22, 23, 24
Castlereagh College,* Montgomery Road, Belfast BT6 9JD
1, 2, 3, 5, 6, 7, 17, 18, 19, 20

North Eastern
Antrim Technical College, Fountain Street, Antrim BT41 4AL
1, 2, 5, 6
Ballymena College, Trostan Avenue, Ballymena BT43 7DN
1, 2, 3, 5
Down College of FE, Market Street, Downpatrick BT30 6ND
1, 2, 5, 6

Larne College of FE, 32–34 Pond Street, Larne BT40 1SQ
1, 2, 3, 5, 6, 7, 20
Lisburn College, 39 Castle Street, Lisburn BT27 4SU
1, 2, 3, 5, 6, 7, 9, 10, 13
Magherafelt College of FE, 22 Moneymore Road, Magherafelt BT45 6AE
1, 2, 5, 6
Newcastle College of FE, 2 Donard Street, Newcastle BT33 0AP
1, 2, 5, 10, 13
Newtownabbey FE College, 400 Shore Road, Newtownabbey BT37 9RS
1, 5, 17, 20
North Antrim College of FE, 2 Coleraine Road, Ballymoney BT53 6DP
1, 2, 5, 6
North Down and Ards College of FE, Castle Park Road, Bangor
BT20 4TF
1, 2, 3, 5, 6, 7, 18, 20
North Down and Ards College of FE, Victoria Avenue, Newtownards
BT23 3ED
1, 2, 3, 5, 6, 7
Northern Ireland Hotel and Catering College, Ballywillan Road, Por-
trush BT56 8JL
1, 2, 3, 4, 5, 6, 7, 8, 9, 10, 11, 12, 13, 14, 16, 18, 20, 22

Southern
Armagh College of FE, Lonsdale Road, Armagh BT6 4TF
1, 2, 5, 6
Banbridge College of FE, Castlewellan Road, Banbridge BT32 4AX
1, 2, 5, 6
Dungannon College of FE,* Circular Road, Dungannon BT71 6BQ
6, 20
Lurgan College of FE, Kitchen Hill, Lurgan BT66 6AZ
1, 2, 5, 6
Newry College of FE, East Campus, Patrick Street, Newry BT35 8DN
1, 2, 3, 5, 6, 7, 18, 20
Portadown College of FE, 26–44 Lurgan Road, Craigavon, Portadown
BT63 5BL
1, 2, 5, 6, 18

Western
Fermanagh College,* Fairview, 1 Dublin Road, Enniskillen BT74 6AE
1, 2, 3, 5, 6, 7, 19, 20
Limavady College of FE, Main Street, Limavady BT49 0EX
1, 2, 5, 6
North West Institute of F&HE, Strand Road, Londonderry BT48 7BY
1, 2, 5, 6, 17, 18
Omagh College of FE, Mountjoy Road, Omagh BT79 7AH
1, 2, 3, 5, 6, 7, 10, 18, 20

Chapter 13
Useful Addresses

Academy of Wine Service
46 Manor Road, Guildford, Surrey GU2 6NQ

The Brewers' Society
42 Portman Square, London WC1H 0BB; 01-486 4831

British Hospitality Association
40 Duke Street, London W1M 6HR; 071-499 6641

British Institute of Innkeeping
51-53 High Street, Camberley, Surrey GU15 3RG; 0276 684449

British Tourist Authority
Thames Tower, Black's Road, Hammersmith, London W6 9EL;
081-846 9000

Business and Technology Education Council
Central House, Upper Woburn Place, London WC1H 0HH;
071-413 8400

Caterer & Hotelkeeper
Quadrant House, The Quadrant, Sutton, Surrey SM2 5AS

The City and Guilds of London Institute
46 Britannia Street, London WC1X 9RG; 071-278 2468

Confederation of Tourism, Hotel and Catering Management
204 Barnett Wood Lane, Ashtead, Surrey KT21 2DB; 03722 77778

Cookery & Food Association
1 Victoria Parade, by 331 Sandycombe Road, Richmond, Surrey
TW9 3NB; 081-948 3870/3944

European Catering Association
1 Victoria Parade, by 331 Sandycombe Road, Richmond, Surrey
TW9 3NB; 081-940 4464

Hotel and Catering Training Company (HCTC)
International House, High Street, Ealing, London W5 5DB;
081-579 2400

Hotel Career Centre
43 Norwich Avenue West, Bournemouth, Dorset BH2 6AJ;
0202 291877

Hotel Catering and Institutional Management Association (HCIMA)
191 Trinity Road, London SW17 7HN; 081-672 4251

Hotel Services Training Unit
David Salomons House, Broomhill Road, Southborough, Tunbridge
Wells, Kent TN3 0TG; 0892 515152

Institute of Food Science and Technology
5 Cambridge Court, 210 Shepherd's Bush Road, London W6 7NL;
071-603 6316

Institute of Home Economics
Aldwych House, 71–91 Aldwych, London WC2B 4HN; 071-404 5532

National Council for Vocational Qualifications
222 Euston Road, London NW1 2BZ; 071-387 9898

Restaurateurs' Association of Great Britain
190 Queen's Gate, London SW7 5EU; 071-581 2444

Royal Institute of Public Health and Hygiene
28 Portland Place, London W1N 4DE; 071-580 2731

Royal Society of Health
RSH House, 38A St George's Drive, London SW1V 4BH; 071-630 0121

Scottish Vocational Education Council (SCOTVEC)
Hanover House, 24 Douglas Street, Glasgow G2 7NQ; 041-248 7900

Scottish Licensed Trade Association
10 Walker Street, Edinburgh EH3 7LA; 031-225 5169

Springboard
1 Denmark Street, London WC2H 8LP; 071-497 8654

The Tea Council Ltd
Sir John Lyon House, 5 High Timber Street, London EC4V 3NJ;
071-248 1024/5

Wine and Spirit Education Trust
Five Kings House, 1 Queen Street Place, London EC4R 1QS;
071-236 3551